Secrets of a New Orleans Chef

Secrets of a New Orleans Chef

Recipes from Tom Cowman's Cookbook

Greg Cowman

University Press of Mississippi
Jackson

www.upress.state.ms.us

Copyright © 1999 by Greg Cowman
All rights reserved
Manufactured in the United States of America

Designed by Todd Lape

07 06 05 04 03 02 01 00 99   4 3 2 1

Library of Congress Cataloging-in-Publication Data

Cowman, Tom, d. 1994.
Secrets of a New Orleans chef : recipes from Tom Cowman's cookbook /
Greg Cowman.
p. cm.
Includes index.
ISBN 1-57806-179-2 (cloth : alk. paper)
1. Cookery, American—Louisiana style. I. Cowman, Greg, 1947–   .
II. Title.
TX 715.2.L68C68   1999
641.59763—dc21   99–31340
CIP

British Library Cataloging-in-Publication Data available

Please e-mail comments to gcart@earthlink.net

Of course, this book is dedicated to the man it is all about, my dear, dear uncle Tom.

But it is also dedicated to the memory of my father, Tom's brother Thayer, who passed away less than seven months after Tom died.

I was, indeed, truly blessed to have been so loved by and close to these two gentle and endearing men.

From the grief and confusion of that desolate year came my decision and commitment to finally put together the cookbook that Tom had talked about doing for so many years.

I sincerely hope the book meets with their approval and that they are toasting it, each other, and me with ice-cold martinis!

Contents

Preface

I first worked with Tom in his kitchen at the Maidstone Arms in East Hampton in 1967. I was nineteen years old, on summer break from architecture school, and ready for a change. Little did I know then that my dear uncle would turn out to be the most influential person in my life.

Tom had a similar effect on almost everyone lucky enough to enter his fold. We all learned much about life from him, whether it was about food, literature, art, travel, or anything else in good taste. He could lead you to taste something exquisite, something you'd never before dreamed you would eat, let alone enjoy. He read voraciously (I don't know when he slept), always passing his favorite books on to friends. His home was an eclectic accumulation of artwork and collectibles that never ceased to surprise and amuse.

When it came to cooking, Tom was as much a teacher as he was a chef. It's impossible to count the number of people he brought under his wing who have gone on to successful careers in the restaurant business. He always gave everyone the chance to learn. He never assigned one repetitious job to do all night long, as is done in many restaurant kitchens. And, as he stressed again and again, it wasn't really important to memorize recipes but rather to understand how the ingredients worked together. This theory applies herein; many of his recipes are merely meant as guides. Use them with this in mind.

Most of the recipes in this book were transcribed directly from his own handwritten papers, ranging from neatly printed sheets from legal pads, to well-worn, food-soiled pages from his sacred recipe "bible," to little scraps of paper he'd squirreled away in books and envelopes.

As is true with any chef, many of Tom's dishes followed him from one restaurant to the next. Occasionally, he would change the names to honor either the current establishment, a local politician or celebrity, or a good friend. But the dish was basically the same. A few of his mainstays: Trout Mousse, Country Pâté, Long Island Duck, Liver à l'Orange, Lamb Curry, Barbados Rum Trifle, and, of course, the Famous Chocolate Cake.

His patrons demanded these signature dishes, and rightly so.

Fortunately, these and many other of his recipes are in this book.

Each year Tom would gather his crew together in front of the restaurant for a staff picture (a few are reproduced in this book). The walls of the kitchen in his home were covered with these photographs. I'd be willing to bet that most folks who worked with Tom kept their copies of these staff pictures too.

The caricature of Tom comes from a large sign I painted for Tom's restaurant in Watermill, Long Island, in the early '70s. I was amazed when Carol Crowley, Tom's dear friend and coworker for many years, brought out the original plywood sign she had been storing for more than twenty years.

I've included pictures of many of Tom's "lovely things," as he used to call them. He surrounded himself with an *olla podrida* of fascinating paintings, sculpture, books, Mexican and Caribbean curios, and—oh yes—even wind-up toys, all of which reflected his characteristic good taste and contagious sense of humor.

Putting this book together has, of course, been a bittersweet matter for me. I've cried more than a few times from missing him, but it's also brought about so many, many fond memories.

Most of my best lifelong friends I know because of Tom. He seemed always to be surrounded by warm, interesting people.

I remember the many places I lived or worked with Tom. The "Fabulous" Hamptons and New Orleans are both such beautiful places. They will always be two of my favorite spots on this earth.

Our six-month sojourn in Mexico was undeniably one of the highlights of both of our lives.

I remember him listening to Ravel, Harry Nilsson, The Who, and Noel Coward, and the funny little sound he made as he whistled along with the music.

There was the lobster and champagne dinner that was so good that we went out, bought two more lobsters and another bottle of champagne, drove home, and did the whole meal all over again.

And then there was the last meal we had together at a local restaurant, when we got so incredibly tipsy, giddy, and loud.

I certainly haven't laughed that hard since.

I am rewarded knowing that this cookbook was something he talked about for a long time. My goal was to make it as much about the man himself as about his wonderful food.

My hope is that, for those people who knew Tom, this book gives them a little piece of him to hold onto again. And, for those who weren't fortunate enough to have felt his presence, a glimpse of the sweet, loving man he was.

Acknowledgments

Because Tom was the man he was, everyone I came in contact with while researching this book had some important input, whether it was a recipe, a picture or two, or a flood of fond memories.

I hold on to each and every one of you now: Mark Benson, Christophe Bergen, Ron Budenich, JoAnn Clevenger, Carol Crowley, John Damark, Loren Dunlap, Donald Gaynor, Charles Bennett Grubb, Mae Grubb, Gary Martin, Audrey Orr, Shirley Ratterree, Deborah Silverman, Deb Skinner, Don "Peaches" Willing (sorry, Don, I couldn't resist), Bill Wright, and someone I only know through e-mail as CyberGlen.

Special thanks are definitely owed to Gene Bourg for his heartfelt introduction. I still get teary-eyed when I read it. Gene wrote the very popular "Eating Out" column for the *New Orleans Times-Picayune* newspaper for many years. He now writes for *Food and Wine*, *Saveur*, and *Gourmet*, and has his own radio show on WBYU. Even though he held the power to turn most restaurateurs into mush whenever he'd review their establishments, in reality he couldn't be a funnier or warmer person. Tom certainly treasured his friendship.

Ever-handsome Louis "Big Lou" Edmonds and his lovely sister Alma Fritchie have been particularly encouraging and generous with their interest and support. If it is possible to have had something good come of Tom's death, it's that I am so much closer to them now.

Jerry Curtis has been an incredible help. He worked with Tom probably longer than anyone else, so it was exactly right that he would review each and every recipe. I feel confident now that they are all correct, or at least as close as they can get (as Tom said, "Remember that a recipe is a list of instructions with something important left out.").

Fortunately for us all, two wonderful people proofread this before it was published. Thanks to Danielle Juzan and John Scheuer.

Thank you to the artists and photographers to whom I am forever grateful for contributing their exceptional work for the enhancement of this book: Mary Cappy, Christine Egan, Mort Kaye Studios, Inc., Becket Logan, Ben Morris, Rise Delmar Ochsner, Norman Parkinson, Cecil Rimes, and Robert Steinau.

And last, extra special thanks must go to Lindy Brown for her immeasurable support and understanding throughout the painful period when I lost both Tom and my father—while at the same time she was bravely fighting (and beating!) breast cancer—and then during the lengthy process of assembling this book. Without her support I'm not sure how I would have gotten through it.

Lindy's favorite Tom story is about when he was vacationing at the beach somewhere, probably in Mexico, and had come from the market with two live lobsters. When he picked up the first one; however, he discovered it was a female, full of roe. Being the kind of man that Tom was, as Lindy tells it, he walked down to the water's edge and released the lobster.

Back in the kitchen, having found the second crustacean roeless and still determined to have his special dinner, he approached the lobster pot. Just as he was about to plunge it into the boiling water he swore he heard the lobster *scream!* So it was back to the beach with that one, too, and poor Tom had vegetables for dinner that night.

Introduction

by Gene Bourg

"Each restaurant kitchen," Tom Cowman once said, "is like a different person."

How typical of Tom to speak even of kitchens in human terms. As much as he loved food and cooking, his friends were always his main sustenance, as well as his greatest joy.

During the last moments he and I spent together, he was in a typical pose, sharing a table with friends, in this case Shirley Ratterree and me, at Begue's Restaurant in the New Orleans French Quarter. It would have been difficult then to decide which he enjoyed more—the sound of our laughter at his delightful stories and observations, or the pork chop he was devouring with a sauce of sun-dried cherries.

"Ah, how good this is with a Pinot Noir," I remember him saying between anecdotes.

In each kitchen Tom used—commercial or domestic—his cooking reflected the diversity of his inspirations. The simplicity of a luscious corn bisque evoked his midwestern roots. Calf's liver with orange sauce could have been from his experiences on Manhattan's or Long Island's sophisticated restaurant scene. His rousingly good *choucroute garnie* probably was taken from the learning experience of a yearlong sojourn in France. The salsas, the moles, and tropical fruit desserts surely were spawned during his frequent vacations in Mexico and the Caribbean.

He was born Thomas Crawford Cowman in Columbus, Ohio. But his palate probably was born in a place like Paris or Cuernavaca. He was a self-taught chef whose early interest in cuisine first blossomed as a hobby.

In 1961 he left a ten-year advertising career in New York City to open his first restaurant, 2-3-4, on East 58th Street, with a friend. Later that year he moved to eastern Long Island, where his reputation grew with Gordon's Restaurant in Amagansett, then was truly made with Tom Cowman's Restaurant in the Maidstone Arms, a resort hotel in East Hampton. The food was good enough to elicit three stars (out of a possible four) from Craig Claiborne, then the *New York Time's* restaurant critic.

In the mid-1970s Tom found his way to New Orleans, where in 1977 he established himself in the kitchen of Restaurant Jonathan, less than a year after the stylish Art Deco establishment had opened on the French Quarter's edge. It was at Jonathan that he began augmenting his already eclectic style with south Louisiana ingredients, especially shellfish, spices, and herbs. After Jonathan closed in 1986, there was a brief stint at Lenfant's, a former New Orleans seafood house (now no more) that had never seen the likes of Tom's sumptuous handiwork. A year later, he joined restaurateur JoAnn Clevenger at Upperline in Uptown New Orleans. In a December 1987 review of the Upperline in the *Times-Picayune* I wrote, "While Cowman's repertory embraces, in varying degrees, the major cuisines of several continents, the elements rarely clash. Everything somehow holds together, in a recognition that food is, after all, one of the few truly universal things we all share." Among the trademark dishes of Tom's that prompted this observation were his cold mousse of fresh trout, that cream-rich corn bisque, a lamb curry that would have drawn praise in Bombay, a tamale with tasso ham and andouille that fairly bellowed with Latin-Louisiana lustiness, a breast of chicken with Thai sauce, a banana-coconut layer cake, and the unforgettable Barbados rum trifle.

Tom also was masterly at interpreting classic New Orleans dishes—barbecued shrimp, gumbo z'herbes, and shrimp rémoulade are the first ones that come to mind. His black-eyed peas with andouille sausage and smothered greens was, in effect, a culinary bear hug.

When he was interviewed by a newspaper reporter in 1977, he likened restaurant dining to theater. "Cooking brings the kind of instant gratification you don't get out of anything but acting," he said. "The restaurant business is so close to theater, except here the curtain goes up at 6 P.M. And nine-tenths of the experience is how the food is presented, how it arrives at the table, the ambiance of the dining room."

But theatrics were not his style. "It doesn't make any sense not to be pleasant," he told the newspaper reporter. "Dishes break, waiters are hassled, the kitchen's hot; but you can get the same things done without having to yell at people."

Yes, people were his sustenance.

Today, in my mind's eye, I see him sitting at his dining room table in New Orleans on Annunciation Street—or Assassination Street, as he liked to call it—presiding like some latter-day Trimalchio over one of those wonderfully endless dinners, constantly checking for empty wineglasses.

I see him on the Zocalo in Oaxaca, ensconced on a café chair under the arches at the Café Le Jardin, the whiteness of his linen suit splashed with the brilliant colors of his bow tie and pocket scarf, sitting there exhilarated by the passing parade on the bustling square under a crystal sky.

I see him shuffling out of a restaurant kitchen and into the dining room, to indulge himself in a few minutes of talk at one of the tables, his brow encircled by that unforgettable bandanna.

I see him standing in my doorway, wearing the most infectious smile a human face can create, carrying under his arm a couple of novels he had enjoyed and wanted to share with me.

I watch him crouched before one of those glorious, glittery *tableaux fantastiques* that, in the last years of his life, he crafted from little wooden boxes, fiddling with the miniature figurines, curios, and spangles to give each construction just the right touch of whimsy or innuendo.

I hear the trumpet of his laughter, erupting from somewhere deep in his heart, while he relishes a funny story.

I feel the touch of his beefy hand on my sleeve as he laughs, his eyes teary with delight.

People say the good die young. I know it's true in Tom's case, because it reinforces the fact of his awesome unselfishness, his unstoppable energy, and his razor-sharp intellectual curiosity. These were but a few of the many gifts Tom gave us. And these were but a few of the qualities that made Tom Cowman, up to the very end, a very young man indeed.

Chef Tom Cowman's Career

1961: Chef of 2-3-4, New York City, New York.

1961–66: Sous chef, then head chef of Gordon's Restaurant, Amagansett, Long Island, New York.

1966: Executive chef of the Bull's Head Inn, Bridgehampton, Long Island, New York.

1967–71: Tom Cowman's Restaurant at the Maidstone Arms, East Hampton, Long Island, New York. Received 3 stars from *New York Times* food critic Craig Claiborne. Claiborne included the restaurant in his 100 Favorite Restaurants of the World.

1969–72: (Winter seasons) Executive chef of the Colony Hotel, Palm Beach, Florida.

1972–74: Tom Cowman's Restaurant, Watermill, Long Island, New York.

1975–76: Executive chef of the Buxton Inn, Granville, Ohio.

1977–86: Chef of Restaurant Jonathan, New Orleans, Louisiana. Received 4 beans (New Orleans-style stars) each year from the *Times Picayune*.

1986–87: Chef of Lenfant's Restaurant, New Orleans, Louisiana. Received 4 beans from the *Times-Picayune*.

1987–94: Chef of Upperline Restaurant, New Orleans, Louisiana. Received 4 beans from the *Times-Picayune*.

Secrets of a New Orleans Chef

Basics

Basics

Beef Stock

Makes about a half gallon

1 pound beef neck or shin bones, cracked	1 whole bay leaf
1 veal knuckle, cracked	6 (or so) black peppercorns, cracked
½ teaspoon salt	½ small white turnip
1 carrot, scraped and quartered	2 cloves
2 medium onions, quartered	½ bunch parsley
1 rib celery with tops, quartered	2 tomatoes, quartered
2 whole cloves garlic	4 beef bouillon cubes

Have your butcher chop the beef and veal bones so that they are open to the marrow. Put them into a 3-gallon pot filled halfway with cold water and add ½ tablespoon of salt. Let stand for an hour or so, then remove the scum from the top.

Add the rest of the ingredients, bring to a boil, then reduce the heat. Let this simmer for at least 2 hours. Skim the scum occasionally, and replenish with hot water to keep the ingredients covered. When cooking time is finished, allow to cool, then strain through cheesecloth or a fine sieve. Clarify* for extra richness. Refrigerate. Remove the fat that has risen to the top (save this for frying or for adding flavor to sautéed vegetables).

To make a richer base for sauces, reduce the stock by boiling. If you desire a deep, dark stock, add caramel coloring.

*To clarify chicken, fish, or beef stock, heat and, before the stock simmers, add 3 egg whites with their crushed shells, stirring all the while until the mixture begins to boil. Let boil for 15 minutes, then strain through cheesecloth or a fine sieve.

Caramel Coloring

½ cup sugar
½ cup water
½ cup boiling water

Dissolve the sugar in ½ cup of cool water in a heavy-bottomed pot. Bring to a boil and cook until it turns dark brown. Add the boiling water. Continue to cook until it is the consistency of syrup. This will keep in a bottle for some time.

MAIDSTONE ARMS   EAST HAMPTON, L. I., N. Y.

Chicken Stock

Tom wrote, "The key to a good chicken stock is chicken, chicken, and more chicken! As in most recipes, these quantities are meant to serve as guidelines, not orders to be followed. *Chacun son goût!*"

Makes about 1 quart

1 cup dry white wine
1 medium onion, sliced
1 cup celery with tops, chopped
1 carrot, chopped
1 whole clove garlic
1 whole bay leaf
4 black peppercorns
¼ turnip, chopped
1 clove
⅛ teaspoon powdered thyme
¼ bunch parsley
2 chicken bouillon cubes
1 3-pound chicken, cut into pieces, no giblets
½ slice raw bacon
1 ¼-pound piece veal or a veal bone (optional)
salt and pepper, to taste

Put everything into a 2-gallon pot and cover with water. The chicken can even be left in one piece while cooking for easier handling, if so desired. Bring to a boil, then simmer uncovered for at least 2 hours, adding water occasionally to keep the ingredients covered. The chicken should be removed as soon as it is tender (20–30 minutes). Remove the meat from the bones and return the bones to the pot. (The meat can be used for many recipes calling for boned chicken, chopped up for chicken patties, or cut up into chunks for chicken salad.) Remove the scum that rises to the top as needed. Taste for salt and pepper after 45 minutes.*

After cooking for about 2 hours, remove from the heat and strain through folds of cheesecloth or a fine strainer. For extra richness the stock can be reduced by boiling and clarifying (see Beef Stock, p. 22). Chill. Remove the fat from the top. The fat can be used for frying or seasoning vegetables.

It's good to make extra stock, as it can be frozen or reduced to use as a base in various chicken dishes.

*Tom wrote, "I think it is best to salt stocks to a minimum until they are at least halfway to completion. As for pepper, one can follow one's own taste."

Fish Stock

This is a good basic stock for sauces and fish stews. It can be frozen.
Makes about 1 quart

¾ pound bones* from any firm-fleshed fish (heads too!)
½ cup onions, chopped
1 small whole clove garlic
1 small whole bay leaf
3 black peppercorns
½ carrot, chopped
½ cup celery, chopped
¼ bunch parsley
1 cup dry white wine
salt and pepper, to taste

Put everything into a 2-gallon pot, then cover with water. Bring to a boil, reduce the heat, and simmer uncovered for at least 1 hour, or until the liquid is reduced to 1 quart. Strain. Clarify (see Beef Stock, p. 22) for extra richness.

*Use shrimp and/or lobster shells to make seafood stock.

Maître d'Hôtel Butter

Make a batch of this and keep it refrigerated (or frozen) for later.

Makes about 4 cups

3 cups soft butter
3 small shallots, minced
2 tablespoons basil, chopped
4 tablespoons freeze-dried chives
2 tablespoons parsley, chopped
2 tablespoons chervil, chopped (if available)
1 tablespoon onion powder
1 clove garlic, minced
1 dash Worcestershire sauce (more, if desired)
1 dash Tabasco (more, if desired)
1 ½ tablespoons lemon juice

Combine all ingredients in a large bowl. (Go ahead, use your hands!)

This goes well with eggs, fish, meats, and vegetables. For example, after pan frying a pepper steak, put a tablespoon or so of Maître d'Hôtel Butter in the pan with a good dash of brandy. *Very* carefully ignite the mixture with a match, let it flame until it burns out, and then pour it over the steak.

Seasoned Flour

You may want to vary the amounts, leave out something, or add something to fit an individual dish. Use this to dust meats, fish, or seafood before browning or sautéing.

Makes about 4½ cups

4 cups all-purpose flour
1 tablespoon dry mustard
1 tablespoon powdered thyme
1 teaspoon chili powder
1 tablespoon onion powder
1 tablespoon paprika
1 tablespoon white pepper
3 tablespoons salt
1 tablespoon cayenne pepper (optional)

Mix everything together in a large bowl. Divide and store in several small paper bags for future use.

Breads

Breads

Chef's Yeast Rolls

Tom was probably one of the few chefs who actually did his own baking. He would purposely wait until the very last minute to bake these heavenly yeast rolls so that the early customers each evening would be greeted at the front door with the wonderful aroma of freshly baked bread.

Makes approximately 2 dozen

1 tablespoon sugar	1 cup lukewarm water
1 teaspoon salt	pinch of sugar
¼ cup lard	8 cups all-purpose flour
1 tablespoon butter	½ tablespoon melted butter
1 cup boiling water	½ cup milk
2 eggs	½ tablespoon poppy or sesame
1 package instant yeast	seeds (optional)

Preheat the oven to 425°. In a large bowl mix together the sugar, salt, lard, and butter. Pour mixture in the boiling water and allow to cook for 2 minutes. Whisk in 1 egg.

Separately, dissolve the yeast in the warm water, sprinkle in a pinch of sugar to activate the yeast, then stir into the mixture.

Sift the flour directly into the bowl a little at a time, mixing gently. Knead the dough until it is elastic and smooth, adding a bit more flour, if necessary.

Pour a little melted butter over the top of the dough (so it won't dry out). Cover with a clean, damp (not wet) towel and put in a warm place to rise until it doubles in bulk, about 1½ hours.

Punch down, then pinch off* the dough and place into greased muffin tins. Brush the tops with an egg mixed with ½ cup milk. Sprinkle the tops with poppy or sesame seeds, if desired. Cover with clean towels and let rise again in a warm place until it doubles in size.

Bake until golden brown, about 15–18 minutes. Remove from the oven and let cool before popping the rolls out of the pans. Warm just before serving.

Make delicious toasties by slicing day-old rolls, brushing with (garlic) butter, and toasting briefly under the broiler.

*To "pinch off," put 2 fingers into the dough and pull up. Then, with the thumb and forefinger of the other hand, squeeze the dough just below the fingers. Try to be consistent!

Hot Tip: Dipping your fingers in some melted lard while "pinching off" helps to keep them from sticking to the dough.

Hot Tip: For cloverleaf rolls pinch 3 small balls (the size of a large marble) for each roll.

Jalapeño Corn Bread

See Garlic Shrimp with Jalapeño Corn Bread (p. 66).
Makes one large sheet pan or about 12 servings

2 boxes Jiffy corn bread mix	½ cup onion, chopped
2 eggs	½ cup green onion, chopped
⅔ cup buttermilk	¼ cup pimiento, chopped
⅓ cup canned creamed corn	½ tablespoon cumin
1 teaspoon garlic, chopped	½ tablespoon onion powder
2 jalapeño peppers, finely chopped	½ teaspoon red pepper flakes
	½ teaspoon salt

Prepare and cook according to the instructions on the Jiffy corn bread box.

Freezes well.

Buttermilk and Chive Biscuits

Makes 18–24 biscuits

2 cups all-purpose flour
1 teaspoon salt
2 teaspoons baking powder
1/4 teaspoon baking soda
1/3 cup Crisco, chilled
3/4 cup buttermilk
1/2 cup cheddar cheese, grated
1 cup fresh chives, chopped, or 1 1/2 cups freeze-dried chives
milk
grated Parmesan cheese
paprika

Preheat oven to 450°. In a bowl sift together the flour, salt, baking powder, and baking soda. Cut in the Crisco with a pastry blender or by slicing with two knives, cutting until the texture is like coarse cornmeal. Make a well in the middle, then pour in the next 4 ingredients, stirring with a fork until the mixture holds together.

Knead on a lightly floured board for 30 seconds (6–7 times). Roll or pat out the dough to ½-inch thick. Cut out biscuits with a cutter or a drinking glass. Place on an ungreased sheet pan. Brush with milk. Sprinkle with a little grated Parmesan cheese and paprika. Bake 12–15 minutes, or until lightly browned.

 Hot Tip: Jalapeño peppers may be substituted for the chives. Use a lesser amount, of course, according to your taste.

Corn and Crab Fritters

Corn and Crab Fritters

Makes about 16 fritters

cooking oil, for deep-frying
1 cup all-purpose flour
¾ teaspoon salt
1 teaspoon baking powder
1 egg, beaten
¼ cup milk
1 small jalapeño pepper, finely chopped
1 cup cooked corn, patted dry, or 1 cup whole-kernel canned corn
½ cup crabmeat, picked clean of shells
Béarnaise Sauce (p. 166)
ketchup or tomatoes, cooked and chopped

Heat cooking oil for deep-frying to 375°. Sift the flour, salt, and baking powder together into a bowl. Add the egg and about half of the milk. Mix until smooth. Add the rest of the milk and mix again. Add the rest of the ingredients and mix well.

Fill a spoon with rounded lumps of the batter about 1½–2 inches in diameter. With another spoon, scrape the lumps carefully into the hot oil a few at a time. When cooked to a perfect golden brown, remove with a slotted spoon to paper towels and drain. Serve with choron sauce (Béarnaise Sauce mixed with a little ketchup or cooked, chopped tomatoes).

Appetizers

Anchovies and Pimientos

Anchovies and Pimientos

This is one of the simplest yet one of the most pleasing first courses.

1 serving

lettuce leaves (Boston, Bibb, or tender romaine)
2 (or more) pimientos*
6 anchovy fillets
1 pimiento-stuffed olive
capers
chopped parsley, for garnish
lemon wedge, for garnish**

Arrange a circular bed of lettuce on a small plate. Place the pimientos on top. Across the pimientos attractively place 5 anchovy fillets. Top with 1 olive wrapped in an anchovy fillet. Sprinkle with capers and chopped parsley. Garnish with a wedge of lemon.** Serve with hot French bread and cruets of good olive oil and wine vinegar.

*If you have the time and inclination, use sweet red peppers that have been roasted in a very hot oven, cooled, skinned, and marinated overnight in House Dressing (p. 110) instead of pimientos.

**A note from Tom on lemon wedges: "When the lemon is quartered, remove the white inner 'vein' and make sure all the seeds are removed. There is nothing more irritating than having to pick seeds out of something before you can eat it. It only takes a second to do this, and it can save tempers." (Anyone who worked with Tom will attest to his obsession with this. He pitched several still-seeded wedges at me over the years.)

Angels on Horseback

Angels on Horseback

1 serving

3 strips raw bacon, cut in half
6 raw oysters, shucked
1 slice soft white bread
Maître d'Hôtel Butter, melted (p. 26)
rice flour or Seasoned Flour (p. 27)
oil, for deep-frying (optional)
lemon wedge, for garnish
parsley sprig, for garnish

To make angels, put half pieces of raw bacon into boiling water until they curl (about 10 minutes), then remove and cool. (This process is called "parboiling." It removes excess fat and will make the bacon easier to wrap around the oyster.) Wrap each oyster with bacon and secure with a toothpick. Refrigerate.

To make garlic croutons, cut a 3-inch round piece of white bread for each serving. Brush liberally with melted Maître d'Hôtel Butter and bake at 350° on a cookie sheet until golden brown.

When ready to serve, roll the angels in rice flour (or use Seasoned Flour, if rice flour is not available), then deep-fry or bake at 400° for a few minutes until the bacon is crisp. Put the garlic crouton on a plate. Stick the toothpicked oysters in a circle on the crouton and pour over some of the melted Maître d'Hôtel Butter. Garnish with a wedge of lemon and a sprig of parsley.

Baked Oysters with Garlic

Baked Oysters with Garlic

8 servings

2 cups heavy cream	more garlic, crushed, to taste
2 cups oyster juice (or clam juice)	2 tablespoons parsley, chopped
	24–32 raw oysters, shucked
1 clove garlic, crushed	1 egg
pinch salt	½ cup milk
pinch white pepper	1 cup (or so) Maître d'Hôtel Butter (p. 26), melted
1½ cups bread crumbs	
¼ teaspoon powdered thyme	paprika
1 teaspoon onion powder	chopped parsley, for garnish
pinch white pepper	lemon wedges, for garnish

Put the cream, juice, garlic, salt, and one pinch white pepper in a heavy, 2-quart saucepan over high heat. Cook down to 1½ cups, about 15 minutes. Set sauce aside. Combine the bread crumbs, other spices, garlic, and parsley. Drain the oysters and pat dry. Combine egg and milk; dip oysters in the mixture. Then roll in seasoned bread crumbs. Place them on a cookie sheet, pour on the Maître d'Hôtel Butter, and dust with paprika. Bake at 400° for 15 minutes, or until brown and crisp. To serve, put some heated sauce on each plate, then 3–4 oysters. Garnish with chopped parsley and wedges of lemon.

Barbecued Shrimp (New Orleans Style)

4 servings

12 large (10–15 per pound) shrimp, with heads and shells on
8 small cloves whole garlic
¼ cup clarified butter*
½ cup water
1 tablespoon Worcestershire sauce
16–20 dashes Tabasco
2½ tablespoons black pepper
1 tablespoon salt
3–4 pinches fresh rosemary
½ cup Maître d'Hôtel Butter (p. 26)
1 twelve-ounce bottle Heineken beer

Sauté the shrimp and garlic in the clarified butter just until the shrimp turn pink (about 2 minutes) and the garlic cloves are slightly brown. Add the other ingredients, except the Maître d'Hôtel Butter and beer, and cook for another 3 minutes. Add the last two ingredients and simmer until the sauce pulls together and becomes creamy. Serve (shells still on) in bowls with hot French bread—for dipping in the wonderful sauce—and with lots of napkins. Or, if you or your guests don't want to deal with the mess, peel the shrimp and serve over angel hair pasta.

*To clarify butter, heat butter until it melts. Remove from the heat. Let stand until the milk solids sink to the bottom. Skim off and save the clear (clarified) butter fat on the top. Clarified butter burns at a much higher temperature, making it better for sautéing.

Celery Rémoulade

Celery Rémoulade

8–12 servings

1 pound celery knobs or
  celeriac (or try jicama!)
milk
1 cup (more or less)
  House Dressing (p. 110)
½ cup good mayonnaise
1½ tablespoons lemon juice
1 hard-boiled egg yolk, sieved
1 tablespoon Dijon mustard

¼ teaspoon tarragon vinegar
¼ teaspoon celery seed
dash Tabasco
generous grind of pepper
salt, to taste
lettuce leaves
chopped parsley, for garnish
lemon wedges, for garnish

Clean and peel the celery, put in a pot, and cover the knobs with a mixture of half milk and half water. Boil until just tender (no more, or they will fall apart). Cool. When cool, cut into julienne strips (about the size of fat kitchen matchsticks). Marinate in House Dressing, overnight if possible. Remove from the marinade and drain.

In a bowl mix together the remaining ingredients (except the last three). Gently toss the julienne celeriac in the sauce, then chill. Serve on a bed of lettuce, sprinkle with chopped parsley, and garnish with a wedge of lemon.

Chicken Empanada with Mole

You can stuff these with just about anything: crabmeat, duck, beans . . .

1 serving

3 slices soft white bread
¼ cup cooked chicken (see Chicken Stock, p. 24)
¼ cup Mole (p. 182)
1 egg
½ cup milk
Seasoned Flour (p. 27)
butter (for sautéing) or oil (for deep-frying)
sour cream
green onions, for garnish
cilantro, for garnish
orange slices, for garnish

Cut 3-inch disks from the bread. Mix the chicken with a little of the Mole, divide equally onto the bread rounds, then fold the bread, pinching the edges together. Rub the edges with a little beaten egg and seal with a fork. Mix the rest of the egg with the milk, quickly wash (don't soak) the stuffed breads, then roll in Seasoned Flour. Fry the empanadas in butter or deep-fry in oil until brown and crisp, remove, and drain well on paper towels. Place them on a plate, pour Mole around the edge of the plate and on top, finishing with a dab of sour cream. Sprinkle with freshly chopped green onions and cilantro, and garnish with orange slices.

I clearly recall the first time I tasted mole. Tom had taken us to a wonderful balconied restaurant in Guanajuato, Mexico. As I supped on a chicken smothered in a delicious, thick, brown mole, we watched the scene below. It was a perfect Saturday night, and the teenagers from town, dressed in their finest, were circling the square (*zocolo*), boys strolling in one direction and girls in the other. It was how they paired off for the evening. (Or, maybe, for life?) Quite charming.

Chef's Pâté

This, I think, is one of the best "country" pâtés.

18 servings

¾ pound lean pork
½ pound fat pork
½ pound veal
¼ pound ham
½ pound chicken or duck
  (for a heavier pâté) livers
1 large onion, roughly chopped
1 whole clove garlic
½ cup milk
2 pieces dry bread
3 eggs
2 small bay leaves,
  broken into pieces
1 teaspoon salt
¼ teaspoon powdered cloves

¼ teaspoon allspice
½ teaspoon thyme
¼ teaspoon nutmeg
½ cup milk
1 cup good cognac
6–8 strips raw bacon
onion, sliced very thin
2 whole bay leaves
lettuce leaves, for garnish
chopped parsley, for garnish
pickled gherkins, for garnish
watercress, for garnish
lemons, for garnish
toasties, for garnish (see Chef's
  Yeast Rolls, p. 30)

Have your butcher grind together the pork, veal, and ham. Place this mixture in a large bowl. Cook the livers in boiling water for 2 minutes, then drain. Put the livers in a blender and add the onion, garlic, and milk. Blend for 1 minute, then empty into the mixing bowl.

Put the next 9 ingredients in the blender. Blend well, then add to the mixture. Now add the cognac and mix well with your hands. Put half of the mixture in a 1½-quart (about 5 x 9 x 4-inch) loaf pan that has been lined with strips of raw bacon. Place a layer of thin (transparent) slices of onion on top. Carefully put the rest of the mixture into the loaf pan. Put 2 whole bay leaves on top. Cover with a double layer of waxed paper and tie securely. Place in a pan of water and bake 1–2 hours in a 350° oven.

Test for doneness by inserting a knife. When it comes out clean, re-move the pâté from the oven and allow to cool slightly. Place a brick (every kitchen should have a brick!) wrapped in foil on top of the pâté. If a brick isn't available, use another loaf pan, weighted down. This removes excess fat and helps the pâté hold together. Chill for at least 24 hours. To serve, cut into ½-inch slices and place on lettuce leaves. Sprinkle with chopped parsley. Garnish each plate with a sliced pickled gherkin, a sprig of watercress, a wedge of lemon, and hot buttered toasties.

Cumberland Sauce (p. 171) and/or good mustard may be served on the side.

This will keep for up to 2 weeks when properly wrapped and refrigerated.

Chutney Eggs with Curried Mayonnaise

4–6 servings

6 eggs
¼ cup Major Grey Mango Chutney, minced
1 teaspoon Pataka's Sweet Lime Pickle, minced
½ teaspoon fresh ginger, grated (optional)
dash Crystal Louisiana Hot Sauce
salt, to taste
lettuce leaves or watercress, for beds
parsley or cilantro, for garnish
pimiento, for garnish

Curried Mayonnaise (Simple)

1 ½ cups mayonnaise (light may be used)
1 teaspoon curry powder (more or less, to taste)
½ teaspoon onion powder
¼ teaspoon ground ginger

Put the eggs in a pot, cover with cold salted water*, and bring to a boil. Reduce to a simmer, then cook for about 15 minutes. Put immediately into ice water** to chill. When cool, peel the eggs and cut them lengthwise. Put the yolks into a bowl and add the remaining ingredients. Mash all together, then stuff the eggs.

On salad plates put beds of lettuce or watercress. Place the eggs stuffed side down, coat with the above Curried Mayonnaise, and garnish with chopped parsley or cilantro and a dot of pimiento on top of each egg for color.

*Salted water makes it easier to peel the shells.

**Ice water helps keep the yolks from discoloring.

Crawfish Cardinal

8 servings

1 cup butter	3 tablespoons Seasoned Flour (p. 27)
½ cup green pepper, finely chopped	2 cups heavy cream
½ cup celery, finely chopped	⅔ small can tomato paste
¼ cup green onion tops, finely chopped	¼ teaspoon cayenne pepper
1 tablespoon shrimp base (if available) or 3 chicken bouillon cubes	½ cup brandy
	1 pound cleaned crawfish tails
	bread crumbs (optional)
	paprika (optional)
1 cup good dry white wine	rice or fettuccine (optional)

Melt the butter in a heavy 3-quart saucepan, then add the vegetables and sauté until soft. Dissolve the shrimp base or bouillon cubes in the white wine, then add to the pot. Mix the Seasoned Flour with the heavy cream, then add to the pot. Stir until the sauce thickens, then add the tomato paste and cayenne pepper. Cook until the flour taste is gone. Add the brandy (and more wine if the sauce is too thick). Remove from the heat and stir in the crawfish tails.

To serve as a first course, put into individual ramekins, sprinkle with bread crumbs and paprika, and heat in the oven. As a main course serve with rice or over fettuccine.

Clams Casino

4 servings

24 cherrystone clams (or try oysters)	2 anchovy fillets, finely chopped
rock salt	½ teaspoon coarse black pepper
1 cup onions, finely chopped	¼ cup sweet butter, melted
1 cup green peppers, finely chopped	1 ½ tablespoons lemon juice
1 small tin pimientos, finely chopped, or 1 cup red bell pepper, finely chopped	2 tablespoons parsley, chopped
	12 strips raw bacon, finely chopped
1 clove garlic, finely chopped	lemon wedges, for garnish
	chopped parsley, for garnish

Steam the clams just until they open. Remove the empty top shells, then place on a cookie sheet that is nearly filled with rock salt.* Mix everything else, except the bacon, in a bowl.** Cover the clams with this mixture. Sprinkle the chopped bacon on top and place under a broiler or in a very hot oven (500°) until the bacon is crisp. Serve immediately with lemon wedges and chopped parsley.

And then there was the customer who had clams on the half-shell.

Upon clearing the first-course plates, the waiter noticed that the man had also eaten most of the bed of rock salt. Barely hiding his alarm, he inquired, "Was everything all right, sir?"

Oblivious to his faux pas, the man replied, "Well, yes, but they *were* a bit salty!"

*The rock salt distributes the heat more evenly, thus preventing the shells from cracking and losing the precious liquid. It also keeps the shells from rolling around.

**Instead of the mixture given here, you could use the recipe for Casino Sauce (p. 169).

Crawfish
Corn Bread Boudin

6 servings

½ cup fish (scraps can be used)

3 tablespoons heavy cream

½ cup crawfish tails

1 egg

1½ tablespoons cold butter

1 large clove garlic,
  steamed or roasted

⅔ teaspoon salt

½ teaspoon onion powder

pinch cayenne pepper

pinch nutmeg (optional)

1 three-inch square piece
  corn bread, crumbled

24–36 crawfish tails,
  sautéed in butter

chopped green onions,
  for garnish

Blend the fish and cream in a food processor for 1 minute. Add the ½ cup of crawfish tails and blend for 30 more seconds. Add everything else but the corn bread, other crawfish tails, and green onions. Blend for 3 minutes. Add the corn bread and blend for 30 more seconds.

Put the mixture onto freezer paper and roll flat (like pastry), about ½ inch thick, so it can be rolled into a cylinder about 2 inches in diameter. Flip the paper and mixture over, keeping the mixture in one piece, and remove the freezer paper. Fill the center with 12 crawfish tails and roll into a cylinder. Put into about an inch of hot (but not boiling) water for 10 minutes. Turn and poach another 12 minutes, then remove and cool. Serve 3 slices per person, topped with the rest of the crawfish tails sautéed in butter and sprinkles of chopped green onions.

Clams Thomas

Tom said, "This recipe could very well be called Clams Rockefeller. However, at the time these were placed on the menu I wasn't feeling too kindly towards the governor, so I called them Clams Thomas."

4 servings

1 ten-ounce box frozen spinach, thawed and chopped	salt, to taste
½ cup butter	8 slices bacon
1 onion, grated small, or 4 shallots, finely chopped	2 tablespoons Pernod (more or less, to taste)
2 tablespoons all-purpose flour	5 dashes Tabasco (more or less, to taste)
1 cup cream	24 cherrystone clams
¾ cup clam juice	rock salt
½ teaspoon white pepper	bread crumbs
½ cup Romano cheese, grated	Romano cheese
¼ teaspoon (a good pinch) powdered thyme	butter
3 egg yolks, separate	paprika
cooking sherry, to taste (optional)	lemon wedges, for garnish

Cook and drain the spinach, squeezing out the excess water. Melt the butter in the top of a double boiler, then add the onion or shallots. Cook for 5 minutes. Stir in the flour, cream, clam juice, white pepper, Romano cheese, and thyme. With a whisk beat in the egg yolks one at a time. (You may at this point add a good dollop of cooking sherry.) Continue cooking and whisking for 5 more minutes or until the sauce has thickened and no longer tastes of flour. Taste for salt and remove from the fire.

Cook the bacon until it's crisp and finely chop it. Combine the bacon with the spinach, then mix into the sauce. Add the Pernod and Tabasco and mix well.

Open the clams and place on a cookie sheet that has been nearly filled with rock salt.* Coat the clams with the mixture. Sprinkle with bread crumbs mixed with grated Romano cheese, dot with butter, and dust with paprika for color.

Bake in a 500° oven until the bread crumbs brown and the sauce bubbles. Serve with a cocktail fork and a large wedge of lemon.

This recipe also works well with oysters. Oysters Thomas (p. 81), however, are quite different.

*See the note for Clams Casino (p. 46)

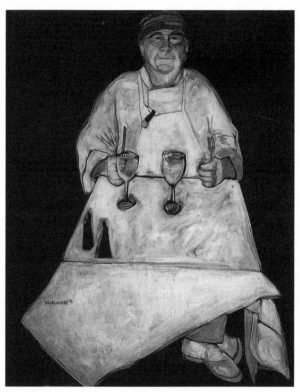

A recent painting of Tom by Rise Delmar Ochsner

Coquilles Imperial

Coquilles Imperial Coquilles Imperial

5–6 servings

2 cups water	¼ cup butter
½ cup cooking sherry	¼ cup all-purpose flour
1 small onion, quartered	pinch powdered thyme
small pinch powdered thyme	pinch white pepper
1 rib celery, quartered	salt, to taste
½ can (5-ounce) clam broth	½ teaspoon (or less) paprika
½ pound shrimp	lemon juice, to taste
1½ cups mushrooms, roughly chopped	½ pound crabmeat, picked clean of shells
1 cup scallion tops, chopped	½ cup pimiento, chopped
1 cup heavy cream	mayonnaise

Put the water, sherry, onion, thyme, celery, and clam broth into a 2-quart pot and bring to a boil. Let boil for 15 minutes or more, strain, and return the liquid to the pot. Bring the liquid to a boil again and add the shrimp. Cook until just done, about 2–3 minutes. Don't overcook!

Remove the shrimp from the stock. Let the shrimp cool a few minutes. Peel and devein (remove the dark matter along the backs). Chop roughly and set aside.

Add the mushrooms to the stock. Cover and simmer for 5 minutes. Add the scallion tops. Cover and simmer 1 more minute. Strain the liquid into another saucepan, reserving the mushrooms and scallions in a separate bowl. Reduce the liquid by boiling to approximately 2 cups, for 5–10 minutes.

To make the Coquilles Sauce, heat (don't boil) the heavy cream in a separate pot. Melt the butter in a double boiler. Slowly stir in the flour, mixing well. Add the reduced stock, again, stirring well. Whisk in the hot heavy cream. Add the thyme, white pepper, and salt. Add some paprika for color and some lemon juice to lighten the taste, then remove from the heat.

In the bowl with the mushrooms and scallions add the cooked shrimp, crabmeat, and pimiento. The mixture should be as dry as possible. Add 1 cup of the Coquilles Sauce and mix gently. In 4-inch scallop-shaped shells (if you can find them) or individual ramekins put about 1 tablespoon of the sauce, then a cup or more of the seafood mixture. Coat the mixture with more Coquilles Sauce, then with a layer of mayonnaise.

Heat at 350° until they bubble and brown. (Or wrap in plastic and heat the next day.)

Serve with rice, *petite pois* (little peas), sautéed cherry tomatoes, and Carrots Vichy.

Carrots Vichy

5–6 servings

10–12 carrots
2 tablespoons butter
6 tablespoons lemon juice
1 tablespoon sugar
salt, to taste

Scrape the carrots and julienne or cut into ¼-inch-thick slices. Put into a 1-quart saucepan. Add the rest of the ingredients and water to cover. Simmer until tender.

Coquilles of Seafood Cardinal

8–12 servings

1 pound scallops	3 tablespoons butter
1 pound small shrimp	4 tablespoons all-purpose flour
¾ cup cooking sherry	½ cup Half & Half
2 cups mushrooms, sliced	½ cup heavy cream
½ teaspoon salt	⅓ cup mayonnaise
¼ teaspoon white pepper	grated Parmesan cheese
1 whole bay leaf	paprika
2 tablespoons scallions, minced	parsley sprigs, for garnish
1½ cups crabmeat, cooked	toasties, for garnish (see Chef's
¼ cup pimientos, chopped	Yeast Rolls, p. 30)

Put the scallops, shrimp, sherry, mushrooms, salt, white pepper, bay leaf, and scallions in a 3-quart saucepan. Cover with water and bring to a boil. Reduce the heat and simmer for 5 minutes. Drain the mixture, reserving the liquid to another saucepan. Add the crabmeat and pimientos to the drained seafood, remove the bay leaf, and set aside. Reduce the liquid by cooking until it makes about 1 cup, about 10–15 minutes.

To make the Cardinal Sauce, melt the butter in a 1-quart saucepan, then add the flour. Stir and cook for 3–4 minutes until thick but not brown. Add the Half & Half, cream, and the reserved liquid. Cook for 5 minutes until thick, stirring with a whisk. Mix ⅔ of this sauce with the seafood mixture. Whisk the mayonnaise into the remaining ⅓ of the sauce.

Spoon the seafood mixture into ovenproof, scallop-shaped baking shells (if you can find them) or individual ramekins. Spread an even layer of the remaining sauce over each shell. Sprinkle with Parmesan cheese and dust with paprika.

Cook at 400° until browned and bubbling. Serve 1 shell as an appetizer or 2 shells as an entree. Garnish with parsley sprigs and toasties.

Pouilly-Fuissé (a dry white Burgundy) rounds out this meal perfectly.

Stuffed Mushrooms

6–8 servings

18–24 large mushrooms	1 teaspoon tomato paste
lemon water	1 cup Beef Stock (p. 22)
½ cup sweet butter	or consommé
6 shallots, finely chopped	cornstarch
½ pound ground ham	bread crumbs
1 cup pimientos, finely chopped	grated Parmesan cheese
½ cup (more or less, to taste)	butter
dry sherry	lemon wedges, for garnish
½ cup parsley, chopped	chopped parsley, for garnish

Remove the stems from the mushrooms. Cut off the tough ends, scrape if necessary, then finely chop. Wash the mushroom caps in lemon water and dry.

Melt the butter in a large skillet, then add the caps and sauté gently, shaking the pan occasionally. Remove the caps. Don't overcook (they should still be firm). Add the stems and the next 7 ingredients and cook for about 10 minutes, thickening with cornstarch mixed with cold water.

Stuff the mushroom caps with the above mixture. Serve hot or cold and garnish with lemon wedges and sprinkles of chopped parsley. To serve hot, mix bread crumbs and grated Parmesan cheese and sprinkle on the mushrooms. Dot with butter and brown under the broiler.

Coquilles St. Jacques

Tom said, "The classic recipe for Coquilles St. Jacques does not call for mushrooms. However, I like them, and they do enhance the flavor."
6–8 servings

1 cup decent (something with a cork!) dry white wine	4 egg yolks, separate
2 cups mushrooms, thinly sliced	½ cup good dry sherry (more or less, to taste)
1 pound bay scallops	bread crumbs
½ cup butter	Parmesan or Romano cheese, grated
1 small onion, grated, or 4 shallots, very finely chopped	butter
2 tablespoons all-purpose flour	paprika
1 cup cream	parsley sprigs, for garnish
½ teaspoon white pepper	lemon wedges, for garnish
¼ cup Romano cheese, grated	

Put the wine and mushrooms in a 1-quart saucepan, cook over medium heat for 5 minutes, then add the scallops. Cover and cook for another 5 minutes. Drain and set the scallops and mushrooms aside, saving the liquid for the sauce.

Melt the butter in a double boiler, add the onion or shallots, then cook for 5 minutes, stirring a few times. Add the flour, stir a couple of times, then add the cream, reserved liquid, white pepper, and Romano cheese. Cook briefly, just until the cheese melts.

Whisk in the egg yolks one at a time. Continue whisking and slowly add the sherry. When the sauce has thickened and no longer tastes of flour (about 10 minutes), remove from the heat and cool. Combine with the scallops and mushrooms.

Spoon the seafood mixture into ovenproof, scallop-shaped baking shells (if you can find them) or individual ramekins. Sprinkle the tops with bread crumbs mixed with grated Romano or Parmesan cheese. Top with small pieces of butter and a dash of paprika.

Put into a 450° oven until brown and bubbling. Serve at once on a plate lined with a paper doily and garnish with a sprig of parsley and a small lemon wedge.

Crabmeat Shostakovich

6 servings

1 pound fresh spinach
1 pound crabmeat, picked clean of shells
1½ cups (or less) Mornay Sauce (p. 183)
6 freshly cooked artichoke bottoms (see Hot or Cold Artichokes, p. 68)
¼ cup hollandaise sauce

Remove the stems from the spinach, rinse well, then chop roughly. Drop it into a pot of boiling water for about 2 minutes, or until wilted. Drain well and squeeze out the excess water. Combine the crabmeat with just enough Mornay Sauce to hold the mixture together.

Remove all of the leaves, the stem, and with a spoon scrape out the choke (the part with the needles) from the bottom of each artichoke. Place the artichoke bottoms into individual ramekins. Put a generous portion of the crabmeat mixture in the center of each artichoke bottom. Surround with a ring of the cooked spinach. Top with a dab of your favorite hollandaise. Put under the broiler for a minute or two, just until the hollandaise turns golden brown. Serve immediately.

According to Jerry Curtis, Tom's right-hand man for more than 13 years, this dish is named after the conductor of the Louisiana Philharmonic Orchestra. It was previously known as Crabmeat Entremont, for the conductor before Mr. Shostakovich.)

Crawfish Tamales

Makes 12 tamales

14 dried corn husks

2 tablespoons lard or shortening

1 onion, chopped

3 cloves garlic, chopped

½ cup red bell pepper, chopped

½ cup green bell pepper, chopped

1 pound cooked crawfish tails (with the fat)

1 teaspoon salt

1–2 pinches cayenne pepper (careful!)

1 cup water or seafood stock (see Fish Stock, p. 25)

salt, to taste

pepper, to taste

2 cups corn flour

½ cup coarse corn meal

½ cup lard or shortening

2 teaspoons lemon juice

4–8 dashes Crystal Louisiana Hot Sauce

Tomatillo Salsa (p. 191)

sour cream

fresh lime juice, to taste

ground cumin, to taste

chopped cilantro, for garnish

Soak the dried corn husks in hot water for at least 1 hour or until they become soft and pliant. (Put a towel or large plate on top to keep them submerged.) Heat the lard in a large skillet, add the onion, garlic, and bell peppers, and sauté until tender. Add the crawfish tails, salt, cayenne, and stock or water. Simmer for a few minutes. Taste for salt and pepper and set aside to cool. (This will be quite spicy at this point, mostly due to the cayenne. But don't worry; it will mellow when added to the corn meal mixture later.)

In a large bowl combine the corn flour and corn meal. In a blender or food processor, blend the lard or shortening until fluffy. Add the cooled crawfish mixture and blend very briefly (don't puree). The mixture should be coarse and chunky. Add this to the corn flour/corn meal mixture. Add the lemon juice and hot sauce. Mix well, adding stock or water, until it holds together.*

Flatten and lay out the 12 softened corn husks. Hand roll the mixture into twelve 4-inch-long cylinders. Place a cylinder in each husk. Tear thin strips from the unused corn husks and tie the ends of the tamales. Put into a steamer or a colander over a pot of boiling water (don't let them sit in the water), cover, and steam for 20–30 minutes, until the tamales are firm.

Serve in the husks, 1 or 2 per person, with generous dabs of Tomatillo Salsa, sour cream mixed with a little fresh lime juice and ground cumin, and sprinkles of chopped cilantro.

*You may then have to add a little corn flour to get the mixture just right. It should not stick to your fingers but should cleanly roll off your hands when shaping the tamales. Keeping your hands damp helps.

The Colony Hotel in Palm Beach, Florida

Deep-Fried Cauliflower

Deep-Fried Cauliflower

Tom said, "This recipe may come as a surprise. It can be served as a vegetable with the entree, as in the case of the Fried Artichoke (p. 63). However, I think it stands very well by itself. The taste is of cauliflower but also a great deal like fried oysters!"

4–6 servings

1 head cauliflower	½ teaspoon salt
milk	oil, for deep-frying
lightly salted water	chopped parsley, for garnish
2 eggs, beaten	lemon wedges, for garnish
2 tablespoons all-purpose flour	kosher salt
½ teaspoon baking powder	Tartar Sauce (p. 192)

Wash and trim a good-sized head of cauliflower, then boil it in a lightly salted pot of half water and half milk. Cook until barely tender, drain, and cool. Break into flowerets and pat dry.

Prepare a batter with the eggs, flour, baking powder, and salt. Dip the flowerets in the batter, then with a slotted spoon drop them into a deep-fryer (or you can use a large, heavy skillet) at medium-high temperature (375°), a few at a time. When they puff and rise to the surface, remove and drain.

Just before serving plunge the cauliflower back into the fryer and cook until nicely browned, then drain on paper towels. Sprinkle with chopped parsley and kosher salt. Serve with wedges of lemon and Tartar Sauce.

Duck Livers Bombay

Duck Livers Bombay

This is a very rich dish.

6 servings

3 tablespoons all-purpose
    flour
2 tablespoons good curry
    powder, plus 1 teaspoon
pinch salt
12–18 good-sized duck livers
    (or chicken livers)
4 tablespoons butter
2 tablespoons onion, grated
1 cup applesauce

1 jar Major Grey (or any good)
    Mango Chutney
2 tablespoons red currant jelly
peanuts, chopped
coconut, grated
red currants, soaked in wine
    or sherry
orange peel, grated
parsley sprigs or watercress,
    for garnish

Combine 2 tablespoons flour, 2 tablespoons curry powder, and salt. Dust the livers with the mixture. Sauté in half of the butter for about 5 minutes, turning often. Remove from the heat. Melt the rest of the butter in a double boiler. Add the onions and cook for 5 minutes, or until they are transparent, then add 1 tablespoon flour and blend thoroughly. Add the applesauce, 1 teaspoon curry powder, chutney, and jelly. Heat and keep this hot, then add the livers about 5 minutes before serving.

To serve, place the livers in the center of a smallish plate. Spoon the sauce over them. Sprinkle with the peanuts, coconut, red currants, and orange peel. Garnish with a sprig of parsley or crisp watercress. If desired, a shaker of curry powder may be passed with this.

Eggplant Provençal

8 servings

2 large (or 3 small) eggplants
kosher (coarse) salt
2 cups best quality olive oil
3 cups onion, chopped
1½ cups celery with tops, finely
   chopped
8 cloves garlic, chopped
5 green peppers, seeded and
   cut into ¾-inch squares
½ pound mushrooms, coarsely
   chopped
2 tablespoons tomato paste
4–5 cups canned Italian
   tomatoes, chopped, or 8–10
   fresh tomatoes, peeled,*
   seeded, and chopped

½ cup raisins
1 tablespoon coarse black
   pepper
2 tablespoons salt
3 tablespoons fresh basil,
   chopped, or 2 tablespoons
   dried basil
½ cup parsley, chopped
½ teaspoon rosemary
lettuce leaves, for beds
chopped parsley, for garnish
chopped basil, for garnish
toasties, for garnish (see
   Chef's Yeast Rolls, p. 30)
lemon wedges, for garnish

Peel the eggplants, slice into ¾-inch thick circles, and sprinkle with kosher salt. Let stand for 30 minutes, then wipe clean. Cut into 1-inch squares.

Prepare the vegetables and herbs as indicated. Heat the oil in a deep saucepan or pot. Add the onions, celery, and garlic and cook slowly for 5 minutes. Add the green pepper, mushrooms, and eggplant. Stir a few times, then add the remaining ingredients. Mix gently, then cover and cook over low heat for 1 hour or until the vegetables are cooked. Taste for salt and seasoning. Chill well.

To serve, put generous portions of the mixture onto flat beds of lettuce and sprinkle with chopped parsley and basil. Garnish with fresh toasties and lemon wedges.

This may also be served as a hot side vegetable, or add extra tomatoes to make an excellent meatless spaghetti sauce.

*Plunge raw tomatoes into boiling water for 1 minute, remove with a slotted spoon, then put in cold water. This makes them easy to peel.

Egg in Aspic

6 servings

1 quart water	4 whole sprigs chervil, or
1 tablespoon vinegar	½ teaspoon dried chervil
1 teaspoon salt	1 whole bay leaf
6 eggs	2 ribs celery, quartered
1 quart rich Chicken Stock	1 large onion, whole
(p. 24)	2 cloves, stuck into the onion
1 cup dry sherry	1 carrot, quartered
12 peppercorns	4 whole sprigs parsley
4 whole sprigs fresh tarragon,	1½ tablespoons unflavored
or ½ teaspoon dried	gelatin, dissolved in water
tarragon	12 fresh tarragon leaves

Put the water, vinegar, and salt in a wide, shallow saucepan and bring to a simmer. Break the eggs one at a time into a saucer and then slide them gently into the hot water. Cook until the white is firm, then remove with a slotted spoon and drain on a napkin. (If they're not going to be used immediately, place them in a pan of cool water.)

Put the remaining ingredients, except the gelatin and tarragon leaves, in a 3-quart pot and boil for 30 minutes. Strain through a fine sieve, then whisk in the gelatin.

Place the eggs in small white ramekins. Crisscross 2 fresh tarragon leaves on top of each egg. Cover with the rich chicken aspic. Chill until firm. Serve in the ramekins with a small spoon.

Figs and Prosciutto

Figs and Prosciutto

As Tom said, "Simple, but oh so good!"

1 serving

2 fresh figs
Boston lettuce leaf
3–4 thin slices prosciutto
lemon wedge, for garnish

Place the beautifully ripe figs, cut into quarters but not separated, on a perfect leaf of Boston lettuce, which is on a lovely hand-painted plate. Put the thinly sliced, rolled up, madly expensive prosciutto beside the luscious figs. Garnish with a generous wedge of plain old lemon.

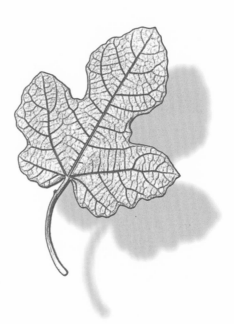

Fried Artichokes

Tom said, "Some prefer this as a vegetable with the main course. Because of its subtlety, I prefer it by itself. I think the result is remarkable!"

1 or 2 servings

1 artichoke
1 cup olive oil
2 cloves garlic, sliced
kosher salt
Rémoulade Sauce, for dipping (p. 187)
lemon wedges, for garnish
parsley sprigs, for garnish

Trim and cook the artichoke (see Hot or Cold Artichokes, p. 68), then cut it neatly in half. Let it drain well, then remove the prickly choke.

In a heavy iron skillet slowly heat the oil. Add the garlic and remove it when it becomes brown. Place the artichoke halves cut side down in the hot oil. Fry for 5 minutes or until nicely browned. Turn, to brown the other side, spooning some of the hot oil into the artichoke. When nicely browned and thoroughly hot (about 8 minutes), remove and drain on paper towels.

Serve warm, cut side up, with a sprinkle of kosher salt or with some Rémoulade Sauce on the side for dipping. Garnish with a small wedge of lemon and a sprig of parsley.

Fried Green Tomatoes

Fried Green Tomatoes

Tom said, "My father loved to eat. He loved to cook, too, but only on festive occasions—holidays or big family parties. Mother cooked the other 360 days a year.

"One of his favorite recipes consisted of not-too-thick slices of green tomatoes rolled in corn meal and sautéed quickly so they were crisp and hot, yet still a little cool inside. This was usually in the fall, when we were buried under tomatoes from the plants he put out in the early summer.

"On top of the golden brown tomatoes he put 2 poached eggs and then, with good, thick, crisp bacon and homemade chili sauce, he would settle in. When Fannie Flagg's *Fried Green Tomatoes* came out, for me it released (like Proust's cookie) memories of my father's recipe."

1 serving

1 green tomato, sliced ½ inch thick
1 raw egg, beaten
½ cup milk
½ cup corn meal
2 eggs, poached (Variation 1)
chili sauce (Variation 1)
Rémoulade Sauce (p. 187) (Variation 2)
3–4 large shrimp (Variation 2)

Combine the egg and milk and dip the tomato slices in the mixture. Coat with the corn meal. Sauté briefly in butter until golden brown (don't overcook!). Put the slices on a plate.

Variation 1: Top with the poached eggs, then the chili sauce.

Variation 2: Peel and devein (remove the dark matter along the back of) the shrimp. Dip shrimp in the egg wash, then corn meal, and fry. Cover the tomato slices with Rémoulade Sauce. Place the shrimp on top of the Rémoulade Sauce.

Fried Whitebait

Tom wrote, "This makes a wonderful hors d'oeuvre or a luncheon dish. The Hotel Plaza in New York served this at lunch occasionally, mixing the whitebait with the tiny oyster crab. A really great dish!"

6 servings

2 pounds whitebait (any small, young fish)	½ teaspoon mace
	½ teaspoon white pepper
olive oil, for deep-frying	¼ teaspoon powdered thyme
vegetable oil, for deep-frying	½ tablespoon paprika
6 whole cloves garlic	kosher salt, on the side
1 ½ cups all-purpose flour	parsley sprigs, for garnish
1 tablespoon dry mustard	lemon wedges, for garnish

Make sure these tiny fish are as fresh and small as possible. Wash well under cold running water, drain, then pat dry. In a deep-fryer or deep iron skillet heat to 350° a mixture of half olive oil and half vegetable oil. Cook the garlic until it begins to brown, then remove. Combine the dry ingredients in a paper bag, add the fish, and shake well, coating the fish with the flour mixture.

Place the dusted fish in a fine mesh deep-fry basket and fry for 3 minutes. Remove and drain on paper towels. Just before serving, plunge the fish back into the hot oil and cook until browned and crisp, about 5 minutes. Drain.

Place on plates and sprinkle with kosher salt. Serve with kosher salt, parsley sprigs, and lemon wedges.

Garlic Shrimp with Jalapeño Corn Bread

4 servings

1/4 cup vegetable oil
1 tablespoon chili powder
1/2 teaspoon salt
1/4 teaspoon cayenne pepper
1 teaspoon garlic, chopped, plus 2 tablespoons
1/2 pound small or medium shrimp, peeled and deveined
1/2 cup mayonnaise
2 tablespoons Dijon mustard
1 tablespoon vinegar
4 three-inch squares Jalapeño Corn Bread (p. 31)
1/2 Bermuda onion, thinly sliced

In a stainless steel bowl blend the oil, spices, and 1 teaspoon garlic. Add the shrimp and marinate for 1–2 hours. Prepare a simple garlic mayonnaise by combining the mayonnaise, mustard, vinegar, and 2 tablespoons garlic (or use the recipe for Aïoli Mayonnaise, p. 102).

Split the corn bread into halves and arrange on plates. Cover the corn bread with the garlic mayonnaise. When ready to serve, heat a medium skillet and add the marinated shrimp and the Bermuda onion. Sauté until done, about 3 or 4 minutes. Divide the shrimp over the corn bread. Serve immediately.

Garlic Shrimp with
Jalapeño Corn Bread

Herring in Dill Sauce

Herring in Dill Sauce

8 servings

½ pint sour cream
½ cup mayonnaise
1 onion, finely chopped
½ cup Dijon mustard
½ cup fresh dill, finely chopped
3 dashes Tabasco
2 large jars Vita Herring in
   Cream

lettuce, for beds
red onion rings, for garnish
chopped parsley, for garnish
toasties, for garnish (see Chef's
   Yeast Rolls, p. 30)
lemon wedges, for garnish

Mix everything in a large bowl. On pretty appetizer plates arrange beds of lettuce. Place generous mounds of the mixture on the lettuce. Garnish with rings of red onion, little sprinkles of chopped parsley, a few toasties, and lemon wedges.

Hot or Cold Artichokes

4 servings

4 artichokes
1 tablespoon salt
1 good dash olive oil
1 good dash white vinegar

Prepare the artichokes.* In a large pot put enough water to cover the artichokes. Add the salt, oil, and vinegar and bring to a boil. Put in the artichokes, cover, and cook for about 30 minutes. They are done when the inner leaves pull out easily or a sharp knife penetrates the bottoms fairly easily.

When done, place in a colander, bottoms up, to drain. If they will be served cold, let them cool, covered with a damp towel, then refrigerate. If they're to be served hot, place them over steam until ready to serve or plunge them into boiling water for a couple of minutes just before serving, draining as above. In either case, be careful not to overcook them.

Hot Artichokes with Chive Lemon Butter

1 cup butter
½ cup sweet (unsalted) butter
½ cup chives, chopped or freeze-dried
1 dash Tabasco
½ teaspoon onion powder
½ teaspoon white pepper
1½ tablespoons lemon juice
salt, to taste
chopped parsley, for garnish
lemon wedges, for garnish

Melt the butter in a double boiler and add the next 5 ingredients. Mix well and taste for salt. Place each hot artichoke in a bowl in the middle of a large flat plate that will be used for the discarded leaves. (Better yet, if you have them, get out those lovely artichoke plates!) Open the leaves slightly and pour the chive lemon butter into the artichoke. Garnish with chopped parsley and lemon wedges.

Cold Artichokes with Red Wine Vinaigrette

½ cup red wine vinegar
½ cup good red wine
1½ cups olive oil
1 tablespoon salt
½ teaspoon white pepper
1 clove garlic, crushed
1 teaspoon onion salt
chopped parsley, for garnish
lemon wedges, for garnish

Combine the ingredients and serve as above.

*About artichokes, Tom wrote: "The artichoke, as you probably know, is the bud of a flower. It is also one of the more ancient vegetables. When tiny, they can be eaten raw in a salad and, when large, the artichoke bottom (also called the heart) can be used in many delicious ways.

"The artichoke should be trimmed before cooking. Leave the stem on until just before cooking, using it as a handle. With scissors cut across each leaf near the top, removing the little thorn at the end of each leaf or petal. Then with a knife cut straight across the top of the artichoke about an inch down. Now you can cut off the stem. The artichoke is now ready to be cooked.

"It's best to wash one's hands after preparing artichokes. The juice can be quite bitter. Also, be sure the pot used to cook the vegetable is scrubbed well after use. How anything with so much gall in it can taste so good is beyond me!"

Hot Sardines with Mustard Sauce

4 servings

1 tomato, thinly sliced	1 teaspoon onion salt
1 onion, thinly sliced	3 tablespoons lemon juice
4 three-and-one-half-ounce cans tiny brisling sardines	grated Parmesan cheese
	cayenne pepper
¾ cup mayonnaise	chopped parsley, for garnish
½ cup Dijon mustard	lemon wedges, for garnish
2 dashes Tabasco	

Arrange layers of tomato slices, onion slices, and sardines (making a "sled") for each serving on a buttered broiling tray. Coat with a mixture of the next 5 ingredients, then sprinkle with the grated cheese and cayenne pepper. Broil until the sauce bubbles and turns golden brown. Remove to individual plates and garnish with parsley and lemon.

Leeks Vinaigrette

4 servings

8 medium-sized leeks
1 cup chicken broth
1 cup (or more) House Dressing (p. 110)
2 hard-boiled egg yolks
capers, for garnish
chopped parsley, for garnish

Trim the leeks by cutting off the roots and most of the green part and peeling away any hard outer leaves. Cut them in half lengthwise, starting an inch from the base so they hold together. Wash them very well in cold water and tie them together with string at the top and bottom into 4 bunches. Cook briefly in chicken broth until tender. Remove and cool, then marinate overnight (if at all possible) in House Dressing.

When ready to serve, place each bundle of leeks on a small plate and carefully remove the strings. Spoon some of the vinaigrette marinade over the leeks. Rub a hard-boiled egg yolk through a sieve onto the leeks. Sprinkle with a few capers and chopped parsley.

Long Island Clam Pie

6–8 servings

¼ pound salt pork, cubed
1 cup onion, chopped
½ cup celery, chopped
1 clove garlic, crushed
1 ten-inch pie pastry top and
 bottom (see recipe for
 Quiche [Basic], p. 84)
2 potatoes, peeled and thinly
 sliced
1 cup small clams, butterflied
 (cut almost in half)

½ cup cream
3 egg yolks (save a little for
 the pastry top)
½ cup clam juice
1 teaspoon cornstarch
pinch pepper
pinch powdered bay leaf
pinch sage
¾ teaspoon salt

Cook the salt pork in a large skillet until it browns, remove (but don't discard it), and pour off most of the fat. Add the onions, celery, and garlic. Cook for 10 minutes or until transparent, then put back the salt pork.

In the pastry bottom put alternating layers of the mixture, potatoes, then clams. Repeat 3 times. Combine the remaining ingredients and pour into the pie. Cover with a pastry top and brush with a little egg yolk. Make 3 steam slits with a knife. Bake at 450° for 10 minutes. Turn the oven down to 350° and bake for another 50 minutes. Remove and allow to cool for a few minutes before serving.

Serve with a broiled tomato and some green peas. Cut the tomatoes in half, sprinkle with bread crumbs and grated Parmesan cheese, then broil until the top browns.

This is also good with scallops or oysters instead of clams.

Melon and Prosciutto

Melon and Prosciutto

1 serving

4 slices chilled, ripe melon, with rind removed
Boston lettuce
3 or 4 paper-thin slices prosciutto, rolled
parsley sprig, for garnish
lime wedge, for garnish

Put the melon slices on a bed of lettuce, lay on the rolled prosciutto, and garnish with parsley and lime.

The Maidstone Arms
ON THE VILLAGE GREEN
EAST HAMPTON, N. Y.   516-324-0390

TOM
COWMAN'S
RESTAURANT
17 ROOMS - 15 BATHS

Twin Bedded Rooms
with Continental
Breakfast For
Two from $19.50

Mushrooms à la Grecque

Mushrooms à la Grecque

6 servings

1 tablespoon orange juice concentrate or 3 tablespoons lemon juice	½ teaspoon leaf thyme
2 cups water	½ bay leaf
1 cup olive oil	12 peppercorns
1 tablespoon balsamic (or white) vinegar	1 tablespoon tomato paste
3 chicken bouillon cubes	1 tablespoon (or more, to taste) Pernod or Herbsaint or 1 branch fresh fennel, if available
1 rib celery, quartered	1½ pounds whole small mushrooms
1 clove garlic, peeled	lettuce leaves, for beds
1 medium onion, quartered	chopped parsley or cilantro, for garnish
½ teaspoon rosemary leaves	
1 teaspoon ground coriander	

Combine everything except the mushrooms in a 3-quart saucepan. Bring to a simmer and cook for 20 minutes. Strain, add the mushrooms, and cook for 5 more minutes. Cool, then refrigerate (overnight, if possible). Serve the chilled, marinated mushrooms on lettuce leaves with a generous sprinkling of parsley or cilantro.

This recipe also works with artichoke hearts, cauliflower, carrots, onions, celery, or a mixture of vegetables.

Mushrooms Paprikash

6 servings

2 pounds button mushrooms

4 chicken bouillon cubes

1 cup cooking sherry

2 cups water

1 cup sour cream

1 tablespoon dill weed

1 tablespoon Grey Poupon Mustard

1 tablespoon hot paprika

Boston lettuce, for beds

lemon wedges, for garnish

melba toast or toasties, for garnish (see Chef's Yeast Rolls, p. 30)

Wash the mushrooms and trim the stems. Combine the bouillon cubes, sherry, and water in a large skillet or heavy, 3-quart saucepan. Bring to a boil, dissolving the cubes. Reduce to a simmer, add the mushrooms, and cover. Cook over low heat for 15 minutes. Remove the mushrooms. Continue cooking the liquid until it's the consistency of a thin paste, then remove from the fire and allow to cool. Stir in the sour cream, dill weed, mustard, and paprika. Put the mushrooms back into the sauce and, if possible, refrigerate for 24 hours.

Serve on beds of Boston lettuce leaves in saucer-shaped champagne glasses. Garnish with lemon wedges and melba toast or toasties.

Mussels in Garlic Sauce

Mussels in Garlic Sauce

Tom said, "The mussel, I think, is one of the best of the shellfish family. It is inexpensive and, in the sea, plentiful. The mussel is as delicate as an oyster and should be treated with respect and, to rephrase a phrase, only cooked to death. They should never be boiled but steamed or baked just until the shells open.

"The mussel needs to be thoroughly scrubbed with a stiff brush and the "beard" pulled out. It should be closed tightly or should close rapidly to the touch, meaning that it's still alive. If it feels suspiciously heavy, discard it as the shell is probably filled with silt and sand."

4 servings

32 mussels, scrubbed and debearded
1 cup mayonnaise
2 hard-boiled egg yolks, sieved
3 cloves garlic, pressed
1 small onion, pressed
1 ½ tablespoons lemon juice
1 teaspoon Dijon mustard
½ cup parsley, chopped
lettuce leaves, for beds
chopped parsley, for garnish
lemon wedges, for garnish

Steam the mussels just until they open, about 8–10 minutes. Let them cool, then remove the empty shell halves. Mix together the mayonnaise and egg yolks. Using a garlic press, press the garlic and onion and add to the mixture. Stir in the lemon juice, mustard, and ½ cup chopped parsley. Coat the mussels with the sauce, then arrange them on beds of lettuce and sprinkle with chopped parsley. Serve with a wedge of lemon and an oyster fork.

Mussels Marinière

Mussels Marinière

8 servings

½ cup butter
1 medium onion, finely chopped
1 clove garlic, finely chopped
3 cups good dry white wine
1 whole bay leaf
1 teaspoon coarse black pepper
8 quarts (about 8 dozen) mussels, cleaned
  (see Mussels in Garlic Sauce, p. 76)
chopped parsley, for garnish
parsley sprigs, for garnish

Melt the butter in a 2-quart saucepan. Add the onion and garlic and cook for 5 minutes or until the onion is transparent. Add the remaining ingredients, bring to a boil, and reduce by ⅓, about 15 minutes. Keep hot.

Place 12–18 mussels per serving (depending on your guests' appetites) into individual baking dishes. Put ½ cup of the mixture into each dish. Put into a very hot (500°) oven and bake until the shells open. Place the baking dishes onto plates. Garnish each dish with a sprinkle of chopped parsley and a sprig of parsley in the middle. Serve with an oyster fork, a soup spoon, and hot bread.

Another way to cook this dish, and perhaps an easier way for the home, is to use a clam steamer or a similar arrangement. Put the wine mixture in the bottom, the mussels in the top. Cover and steam until the mussels open. Divide them into soup bowls and pour over the liquid. Serve as described above.

Mussels Ravigote

8 servings

1 cup onion, chopped	2 tablespoons sour pickles, finely chopped
1 cup dry white wine	½ teaspoon tarragon leaves, crushed
1 cup water	1 teaspoon tarragon vinegar
dash white pepper	1 tablespoon Dijon mustard
8 quarts (about 8 dozen) mussels, cleaned (see Mussels in Garlic Sauce, p. 76)	crushed ice, for beds
2 cups mayonnaise	paprika
3 tablespoons pimiento, finely chopped	chopped parsley, for garnish
2 tablespoons chives or green onion tops, chopped	lemon wedges, for garnish

Put the onion, wine, water, and pepper in 6-quart pot. Bring to a boil, then add the mussels and cover. Remove them as they open, after about 8–15 minutes, stirring the pot occasionally to bring opened ones to the top. When cool, remove one shell from each mussel and loosen each mussel in its second shell. Combine the remaining ingredients and mix well. Coat the mussels in the shells with this sauce. If possible, serve on beds of crushed ice. Dust with paprika and sprinkle with chopped parsley. Garnish with lemon wedges.

Onion Sandwiches

Tom said, "This may sound like a strange dish, but these are truly delicious. Surprise your guests at your next party!"

16 finger sandwiches

1 Bermuda onion, thinly sliced
salt
lime juice
4 slices soft white or wheat bread (or use both)
½ cup softened butter or margarine
¼ cup cilantro, chopped
¼ cup tomatoes, chopped
watercress, for garnish

Put the onions in a bowl and salt well. This takes out the strong flavor. After a little while, rinse well in cold water. Put the onions into dry, clean towels, then gently squeeze out the water. (Don't bruise the onions, though!) Sprinkle with a little freshly squeezed lime juice. Toss gently.

Lay out the bread and spread with a thin layer of butter or margarine. This prevents the bread from getting soggy. Put the onions on next. Sprinkle with chopped cilantro and chopped tomatoes. Cover with another piece of buttered bread. Carefully cut off the crusts and cut into small triangles. Refrigerate briefly. Serve on a platter and garnish with sprigs of watercress.

As Tom said, "You won't believe it!"

Onions Stuffed with Vegetables

8 servings

4 large onions (a little smaller than softballs)

6 carrots, diced small

2 medium-sized turnips, diced small

1 box frozen peas, thawed

1 cup (or less) Cream Sauce (p. 170)

mayonnaise

bread crumbs

grated Parmesan cheese

paprika

Peel the onions, cut them each in half, and put them in a roasting pan with the cut side down. Cover halfway with water and bake at 350° for 30 minutes. After cooking, take the onions out of the pan, turn them over, and allow to cool. When they're cool take out most of the center, leaving a cup shape for stuffing and saving the portion removed to one side.

While the onions are cooking, prepare the carrots and turnips, then cook in salted water until tender. Drain and put in a bowl. Add the onion centers (chopped) and the peas. Bind the mixture together with Cream Sauce. Fill the onion cups with the vegetable mixture. Lightly coat with mayonnaise and sprinkle with bread crumbs, grated Parmesan cheese, and paprika for color. Bake at 350° for 30 minutes. Serve as an appetizer or as a side dish with any entree.

Oysters Thomas

4 servings

16 oysters on the half shell
rock salt
2 cups Béarnaise Sauce (p. 166)
2 cups Cream Sauce (p. 170)
1 pound lump crabmeat, picked clean of shells
1 cup bread crumbs
paprika
lemon wedges, for garnish
parsley sprigs, for garnish

Wash the oyster shells and place on a bed of rock salt in a flat pan.
Into each shell put 1–2 teaspoons of Béarnaise Sauce. Place an oyster
on top, then some crabmeat. Mix the remaining Béarnaise Sauce with
the Cream Sauce and cover the oysters and crab. Sprinkle with bread
crumbs and dust lightly with paprika. Bake at 400° for 15 minutes or
until the sauce bubbles and turns brown. Serve with wedges of lemon
and sprigs of parsley.

Oyster Stuffings

Each of the following recipes will make about 8 servings with 6 oysters per person.

Aïoli and Lime

3 cups mayonnaise

¼ cup lime juice

3 cloves garlic, blended

I egg yolk

¼ tablespoon dry mustard

2 tablespoons Grey Poupon
   Mustard

¼ tablespoon onion powder

⅛ tablespoon white pepper

½ cup bread crumbs

salt, to taste

grated Parmesan cheese

paprika

Combine everything except the grated cheese and paprika. Put a little sauce into each oyster shell, then an oyster, then more sauce on top. Sprinkle on the grated cheese and paprika. Heat in a 400° oven until the sauce bubbles around the edges.

Shrimp and Tomato

I pound boiled shrimp, peeled
   and deveined

¼ cup butter

2 bunches (about I cup)
   scallions, white and green
   parts, chopped

¼ cup all-purpose flour

I tablespoon lobster base, if
   available, or 3 fish bouillon
   cubes

2 tablespoons tomato paste

¼ cup lemon juice

¼ cup fresh basil, chopped

½ tablespoon onion powder

¼ teaspoon white pepper

2 dashes Tabasco

2 cups tomatoes, diced

chopped parsley, for garnish

sliced black olives, for garnish

Put the shrimp in boiling water for 2–3 minutes. Peel and devein (remove the dark matter along the back), then chop fine. Melt a little of the butter in a large skillet, cook the scallions for a few minutes, then remove. Melt the rest of the butter in the skillet, add the flour, and cook until the flour is absorbed. Add everything else, putting the tomatoes in last. Cook for a few minutes, then add the shrimp and scallions. Taste for salt.

Put a little mixture into each oyster shell, then an oyster, then more mixture on top. Heat in a 400° oven until the sauce bubbles around the edges. Garnish each oyster with a sprinkle of chopped parsley and a cross of sliced black olives.

Spinach, Bacon, and Mushrooms

1 pound frozen leaf spinach	1 cup water
1 pound bacon	pinch ground thyme
1 pound mushrooms, chopped medium-fine	good pinch cracked pepper
½ cup butter	½ teaspoon onion powder
¼ cup all-purpose flour	2 dashes Tabasco
1 tablespoon tomato paste	¼ cup lemon juice
1 tablespoon clam base, if available, or 3 fish bouillon cubes	Pernod or Herbsaint to taste (optional)
½ cup cooking sherry	olive slices, for garnish
	pimiento strips, for garnish

Thaw and cook the spinach, drain well (squeeze the excess water out, if necessary), and chop roughly. Cook and finely chop the bacon. Melt a little of the butter in a large skillet. Briefly sauté the mushrooms, then remove.

Melt the rest of the butter in the skillet, add the flour, and cook until the flour is absorbed. Add the remaining ingredients and cook until the sauce is thick with no lingering flour taste.

Combine the sauce with the spinach, bacon, and mushrooms. Put a little of the mixture into each oyster shell, then an oyster, then more mixture on top. Garnish with a slice of olive and a small strip of pimiento. Heat in 400° oven until the sauce bubbles around the edges.

Quiche (Basic)

Pastry

6–8 nine-inch pie shells
1 cup lard
1/2 cup butter or margarine
4 hard-boiled egg yolks, sieved
8 cups pastry or cake flour
1 1/2 tablespoons baking powder
3/4 tablespoon salt

Combine the lard and butter in a high-sided bowl. Whip until well blended. Add the egg yolks and blend well. Sift the flour, baking powder, and salt together into another bowl. Mix with the butter/egg mixture until it's like corn meal (more flour may be needed). Sprinkle with cold water, 1/8 cup at a time, and mix until it forms a rollable pastry. (Be careful with the water! The dough should barely hold together when made into a ball.)

This can be divided, wrapped in freezer paper, and frozen.

Basic Filling

1 pie

5 large eggs
1 cup heavy cream
2 cups Half & Half
1/4 teaspoon white pepper
1/4 teaspoon powdered thyme
2 tablespoons freeze-dried chives
2 tablespoons cooking sherry
1/2 teaspoon onion powder
1 cup Swiss cheese, grated

pinch salt	paprika
grated Parmesan cheese	parsley sprigs, for garnish
chopped parsley	broiled tomatoes, for garnish

Mix the first 10 ingredients in a large bowl, then pour into the pie shell. Sprinkle with grated Parmesan cheese and chopped parsley, then dust lightly with paprika. Bake at 325° for 45 minutes or until the liquid sets. Cool slightly before serving. Serve in wedges. Garnish with parsley and broiled tomatoes.

You can add just about anything to a quiche: spinach, mushrooms, bacon, shrimp, crab, crawfish, lobster, oysters, clams, onions, anchovies, artichoke hearts, olives, etc. Depending on the additions, you may have to reduce the amount of liquids and adjust the spices.

The Maidstone Arms
TOM COWMAN'S RESTAURANT
TODAY

White Asparagus with Prosciutto	3.50
Mushrooms stuffed with Crab Remoulade	3.75
Avocado Vinaigrette or	
stuffed with Ceviche	3.50
Ham & Spinach Quiche Pernod	3.25
Clams steamed in Wine and Tomato	4.25

Puree of Bean Sherry	1.75
Chicken Broth Oaxaca	1.75
Iced Cream of Water cress	2.25

Cold poached Bass w/ fresh Ginger - Garni	10.25

Broiled local Bluefish or Bass	8.50
Sole with Lobster and White Grapes	10.50
Sauté Breast of Lemon Chicken - Pilaf	8.50
Sauté of Veal à la Marengo	9.25
Roast Filet of Beef au Poivre Vert	10.50

Apple Tart with fromage de Brie	2.75

Potato   Fresh Vegetable

Green Salad: Dijon—Vinaigrette
Blue Cheese or Russian Dressing 1.75

Burgundy, Chablis, Rose by the Carafe
9 oz. 3.00   18 oz. 5.75

Vintage Wines Available

We Regret, No Credit Cards

Quiche Lorraine

This may be served hot or cold. With a small salad it makes a wonderful light lunch or late supper.

6–8 servings

1 nine-inch pie pastry (see Quiche [Basic], p. 84)	4 eggs
3 scallions, white and green parts, finely chopped	1 cup heavy cream
	1 teaspoon salt
6 strips crisp bacon, chopped, or 1 cup fried ham, diced, or a combination of the two	½ teaspoon coarse black pepper
	½ cup cooking sherry
2 ounces Camembert cheese, pushed through a sieve	¼ cup parsley, chopped
	1 small dash nutmeg (optional)
¾ cup Swiss cheese, grated	paprika
	parsley sprigs, for garnish
4 anchovy fillets, finely chopped	tomatoes, broiled, for garnish

Line a pie plate or tart pan with the pastry. Put in the scallions, bacon, cheese, and anchovies. Combine the next 7 ingredients and pour into the crust. Dust with paprika and bake for 15 minutes in a 425° oven. Reduce the heat to 350° and cook another 45 minutes or until the liquid sets. Let cool for a few minutes before cutting. Serve in wedges with sprigs of parsley and broiled tomatoes.

Quiche with Seafood

Quiche with Seafood

As with the Quiche Lorraine, this may be served hot or cold. It too makes a lovely lunch or supper dish.

6–8 servings

1 nine-inch pie pastry (see
  Quiche [Basic], p. 84)
4 scallions, white and green
  parts, finely chopped
1 cup chunked lobster,
  crabmeat, scallops, shrimp,
  mussels, or any combination
  of these
2 anchovy fillets, finely chopped
4–5 eggs (depending on size)
1 cup heavy cream
1 teaspoon salt
½ teaspoon coarse black
  pepper
1 dash nutmeg or mace
  (optional)
½ cup cooking sherry
½ cup grated Parmesan cheese
¼ cup parsley, chopped
paprika
parsley sprigs, for garnish
broiled tomatoes, for garnish

Line a pie plate or tart pan with the pastry. Put in the scallions, seafood, and anchovies. Combine the next 8 ingredients and pour into the crust. Dust with paprika and bake for 15 minutes in a 425° oven. Reduce the heat to 350° and cook another 45 minutes or until the liquid sets. Let cool for a few minutes before cutting. Serve in wedges and garnish with parsley sprigs and broiled tomatoes.

Serve with a small garden salad or fresh fruit salad.

Roasted Garlic

10 servings

10 whole heads garlic
2 tablespoons extra virgin olive oil
2 tablespoons vegetable oil
1 tablespoon fresh thyme leaves (or try other herbs)
1 tablespoon kosher salt
½ teaspoon black pepper, freshly ground

Cut off the top third of each head of garlic. Combine the other ingredients in the bottom of a small, shallow baking dish, then put in the garlic pods, cut side down. Roast for 35 minutes at 350° or until the cloves are soft and the cut edges are slightly caramelized. Squeeze the pod to extract the now spreadable garlic cloves.

This is delicious on French bread, with grilled fish or meats, in sauces for pasta or vegetables, or in salad dressings.

Tom had a funny story about garlic: "In the early 1950s there were six young Americans living in Paris on very little money. By the end of the month we would scrounge (it's the only word to use) around Les Alles for a carrot here, a little lettuce, an onion there. But our mainstay was pasta bordelaise (garlic, oil, and parsley). We didn't notice that people were probably edging away from us . . .

"Bill Raidy, a rich friend, came to town and checked into the Ritz. It was midwinter and very cold, and the bath in our hotel was even colder, so we put on our best, took our kit bags and went to the Ritz to bathe. Bill went to have lunch with a friend while we abluted.

"Returning, he opened the door to his room and, as he said later, it was as if he had been engulfed in a cloud of garlic. He had to change hotels and have all his clothes laundered, and to this day, just the mention of garlic will set him off. But, oh, that bath!"

Roasted Red Bell Peppers
with Anchovies and Capers

Roasted Red Bell Peppers
with Anchovies and Capers

6 servings

½ cup olive oil
6 red bell peppers
12 cloves garlic, peeled
kosher salt
36–48 anchovy fillets
capers
Italian parsley sprigs, for garnish

Pour the oil onto a sheet pan. Cut each pepper in half and remove the internal membranes and seeds. Rub the peppers with some of the olive oil. Place them cut side down on the pan. Put a clove of garlic under each pepper half. Sprinkle with a little kosher salt. Put in a 400° oven for 15 minutes or until the skin blackens. Remove and cover with foil and let cool. The skin can now be removed, if desired.

Place the roasted peppers attractively on salad plates. Make a cross-hatch design of anchovy fillets on top of each pepper and sprinkle with capers. Garnish with sprigs of Italian parsley. Pass cruets of good quality olive oil and vinegar and a pepper grinder. Serve with hot French bread.

Scampi Rémoulade

"Scampi, as you may know, are deep sea shrimp that are caught off the shores of the Balearic Islands. They come in 5-pound boxes and are expensive ($8.50 for a box of approximately 48 shrimp). They are large, about 3 inches long, and fat. They have a distinctive red color and are much sweeter than the usual 'jumbo' shrimp." (This recipe was taken from Tom's writings recorded in 1964, thus the interesting price quote.)

4–6 servings

4–5 black peppercorns
½ onion, sliced
1 whole bay leaf
tops from ½ stalk celery, with leaves
1–2 large sprigs parsley
2½ pounds scampi, thawed, if necessary
lettuce, for beds
1–2 cups Rémoulade Sauce (p. 187)
lemon wedges, for garnish
chopped parsley, for garnish

Put the peppercorns, onion, bay leaves, celery, and parsley in a 3-gallon pot filled halfway with water. Bring to a boil and cook for 20 minutes. Add the scampi, bring back to a boil, and cook for 5 minutes. Remove and drain, then cool under cold running water.

Peel and devein the scampi (remove the dark matter along the backs). On flat beds of lettuce arrange 4 or more scampi, slightly overlapping, then cover with Rémoulade Sauce. Top with scampi, cut in half lengthwise, and garnish with lemon wedges and sprinkles of chopped parsley.

Sherried Mushrooms with Garlic

Tom said, "This is wonderful as an appetizer or on the side with filet of beefsteak or chicken. Or add some reduced (thickened and condensed by cooking) cream for a lovely pasta sauce."

4 servings

3 tablespoons olive oil

6 cloves garlic, sliced paper-thin

1 pound trimmed mushrooms, sliced or quartered

½ cup dry sherry

3 tablespoons lemon juice

1 chicken bouillon cube, dissolved in a little water

1 teaspoon Worcestershire sauce

1 teaspoon paprika

pinch powdered thyme

few dashes Louisiana hot sauce

½ cup parsley, chopped (save a little for garnish)

cornstarch

sherry

salt and pepper, to taste

Heat the oil in a heavy, 2-quart saucepan. Add the garlic and cook for 2 minutes. Add the mushrooms, mix well, then add the next 8 ingredients. Cook for 10 minutes, stirring often. Bind the sauce with a little cornstarch dissolved in sherry. Taste for salt and pepper. Sprinkle with chopped parsley.

Hot Tip: To make the sauce extra good, combine domestic mushrooms with some wild mushrooms, or smoke the mushrooms first.

Seafood Cakes

8 servings

½ pound firm-textured fish (drum, salmon, etc.)
½ pound shrimp, roughly chopped
12 slices white bread, with crust removed
1 cup good quality olive oil
4 egg yolks (set aside the whites)
1 teaspoon dry mustard
½ teaspoon salt
¾ teaspoon paprika
1 tablespoon Worcestershire sauce
1 cup celery, finely chopped
½ cup onions, finely chopped
½ cup pimientos, finely chopped
oil or clarified butter (see Barbecued Shrimp, p. 39), for sautéing
¼ pound fresh spinach, cut into thin strips, blanched,* and drained
½ pound lump crabmeat, picked clean of shells
1 cup green onion tops, finely chopped
4 egg whites, whipped until stiff
1 cup (or more) Red Bell Pepper Sauce (p. 186)
cilantro sprigs, for garnish
lemon or lime wedges, for garnish

Poach the fish and shrimp by cooking it briefly in simmering water or Fish Stock (p. 25).** Set aside to cool. Arrange the bread on a cookie sheet and pour on the oil. Let the bread absorb the olive oil (for about 30 minutes), then pull it apart into "lump crab"-sized pieces (½-inch squares).

In a bowl mix the egg yolks, mustard, salt, paprika, and Worcestershire sauce. Add the bread pieces and toss lightly. Sauté the celery, onions, and pimientos in a little oil or clarified butter until tender, then combine with the bread mixture.

Break the fish into small flakes and add to the mixture. Add the spinach, crabmeat, green onion tops, and shrimp, tossing gently. Fold in the egg whites. Form into 4-inch diameter cakes. Sauté in very little oil or clarified butter. When nicely browned, remove and drain on paper towels.

Put some Red Bell Pepper Sauce onto each plate, then put 2 hot seafood cakes on the sauce. Serve with sprigs of cilantro and lemon or lime wedges.

*To blanch spinach, plunge the fresh spinach leaves into boiling water for about 2 minutes. Remove and drain well. This preserves the green color of the spinach and removes the excess water within (sometimes called "wilting"), which lets it hold together with the other ingredients. Also, one doesn't want the water escaping during the final step of sautéing the cakes.

**To poach fish, put enough water or Fish Stock to cover the fish into a heavy, flat-bottomed roasting or baking pan (or a real poaching tray, if you have one). If using thin, delicate fish, first bring the liquid to a simmer, then, using a large spoon or flat metal spatula, very carefully slide in the fish. For thicker, firmer fish, start in cold liquid, bring just to a boil, then immediately reduce to a simmer. Spoon some of the hot liquid over the fish to ensure thorough cooking. The fish is done when it is opaque all the way through (check by parting the flesh slightly), about 5–8 minutes per pound (depending on the thickness of the fish) from the time it begins simmering. Remove with a slotted spoon or other such utensil. Do not let it cool in the liquid.

Shrimp and Grits

4 servings

2 tablespoons peanut oil
⅓ pound bacon, chopped
1½ cups mushrooms, sliced
1½ cups green onions,
  chopped
2 teaspoons garlic, chopped
2 teaspoons lemon juice
⅓ cup parsley, chopped
2 teaspoons Tabasco
1–2 dashes Worcestershire
  sauce
1 pound boiled shrimp, peeled,
  deveined, and halved
4 servings grits

Heat the oil in a large skillet, then add everything but the shrimp and grits. Cook until the onions and garlic are cooked and the bacon is browned (not crisp), about 5–6 minutes. Add the shrimp and heat until hot. Serve over grits.

The 1988 staff at Upperline Restaurant, New Orleans

Soft-shell Crabs with Thai Sauce

4 servings

4 soft-shell crabs
1 egg, beaten
½ cup milk
1 cup Seasoned Flour (p. 27)
oil, for deep-frying
lettuce leaves, for beds
2 bananas, sliced
2 cups Spicy Thai Sauce (p. 190)
chopped cilantro and sprigs, for garnish
lemon wedges, for garnish

Clean the crabs (or have your fishmarket person do it if you are squeamish). With a sharp knife or scissors cut off the eyes (this kills the crab instantly—there's not even time for it to scream!) and trim away the tail. Lift the pointed ends to reveal the soft, spongy gills. Scrape this material out. Rinse well and pat dry.

Dip each crab into a mixture of egg and milk, then dust with Seasoned Flour. Holding the crab body with tongs so that the legs are hanging down, lower just the legs into a hot deep fryer, cooking them until they are golden brown. Turn the crab over and cook the body to match the legs.

Put the cooked crab on a bed of lettuce on a plate with the legs up and fill the center with sliced bananas. Cover generously with Spicy Thai Sauce. Garnish with chopped cilantro, sprigs of cilantro, and lemon wedges.

Spanish Crawfish
Spanish Crawfish

1 serving

2 tablespoons olive oil

2 tablespoons Maître d'Hôtel Butter (p. 26)

2 clóves garlic, sliced

tiny pinch saffron

12–15 live crawfish

1 tablespoon kosher salt

2 tablespoons brandy

1 tablespoon parsley, chopped

Heat the oil and butter in a skillet, add the garlic and saffron, and cook until the garlic is soft, about 5 minutes. Add the crawfish, sprinkle in the kosher salt, cover, and shake (the pan, silly!). Cook for a few minutes, still shaking the pan, until the crawfish take on color. Add the brandy and parsley, cover, and cook 5 more minutes.

Stuffed Eggplant

Stuffed Eggplant

8 servings

4 small eggplants	2 teaspoons sugar
salt	½ tablespoon coarse black
I cup good quality olive oil	pepper
2–3 tablespoons lemon juice	2 tablespoons chopped fresh
I½ cups onions, chopped	basil or I tablespoon dried
5 cloves garlic, chopped	basil
I cup celery, chopped	I teaspoon dried oregano
24 medium mushrooms,	bread crumbs
chopped	grated Parmesan cheese
5 cups tomatoes, peeled (see	24 anchovy fillets
Eggplant Provençal, p. 60),	paprika, for color
seeded, and chopped	chopped parsley and sprigs,
I tablespoon salt	for garnish

Cut each eggplant in half lengthwise and make slits in the pulp ¼ inch deep. Open the slits and sprinkle with salt. Let stand for 30 minutes, then squeeze out the liquid and dry with a clean cloth. Brush with a little olive oil. Arrange the eggplant cut side down on a baking sheet and bake at 375° for 45 minutes. Remove from the oven and cool.

When cool, scoop out the pulp, leaving the skin intact. Chop the pulp coarsely. Sprinkle with lemon juice to prevent discoloring. Heat the oil in a deep 2-quart pot. Stir in the eggplant, onions, garlic, celery, mushrooms, tomatoes, and seasonings. Stir well.

Cover and cook slowly for 1 hour, stirring occasionally. Remove from the fire and cool. When cool, stuff the eggplant shells with the mixture. Sprinkle with a mixture of half bread crumbs and half grated Parmesan cheese. Put 3 anchovy fillets across each stuffed shell, sprinkle with paprika, then heat at 400° until the tops are golden brown. Garnish with chopped parsley and parsley sprigs.

Trout Mousse

This was one of Tom's most famous dishes and was probably included on the menu of each of his restaurants. People still talk about it!

12–16 servings

1 quart water	1 tablespoon onion powder
1 cup cooking sherry	1 tablespoon gelatin,
1 onion, roughly chopped	dissolved in
1 whole bay leaf	2 tablespoons tarragon vinegar
3 ribs celery, roughly chopped	black olive slices, for decoration
2 tablespoons plain gelatin	pimento slices, for decoration
salt and white pepper, to taste	fresh dill leaves, for decoration
1 pound trout (flounder or sole	Boston lettuce or, preferably,
can be used instead)	watercress
1 cup mayonnaise	lemon wedges, for garnish
1 tablespoon lemon juice	parsley, for garnish
2 tablespoons Dijon mustard	cherry tomatoes, for garnish
½ teaspoon tarragon leaves,	toasties (see Chef's Yeast Rolls,
crushed	p. 30)
1 teaspoon dill weed	Dill Mayonnaise (p. 107)
½ teaspoon white pepper	

Put the water, sherry, onion, bay leaf, celery, gelatin, and salt and pepper in a 2-quart pot and boil for 15 minutes or more. Put the fish in another pot and strain the stock over it. Let the fish poach (see Seafood Cakes, p. 92) for a few minutes until it flakes (don't overcook), then remove and let it cool a bit. Strain the liquid into another pot (yes, that's 3 pots so far). Gently flake the fish into a bowl over ice, then pour in 1 cup of the stock. While the fish is cooling, clarify (see Beef Stock, p. 22) and cool the remaining stock to use as a clear aspic.

In the bowl with the cooled fish whip in the next 9 ingredients. The mixture should have a smooth, light texture. Pour ¼ inch of the cooled, clarified aspic into a 3-quart mold (or you can use individual ramekins) and chill to firm slightly. Decorate with black olive and pimento slices and fresh dill leaves, then carefully pour in more aspic. Chill again to firm. When firm, fill the mold with the fish mixture, wrap with plastic wrap, and refrigerate for about an hour, until firm.

Put the mold down into warm water for a few seconds, run a knife along the edge, and invert it onto a bed of Boston lettuce or watercress on a chilled platter. Remove the mold.

Serve whole at a party or sliced as individual appetizers. Garnish the platter or plates with lemon wedges, parsley sprigs, cherry tomatoes, and 3 or 4 fresh toasties per person. Put a dab of Dill Mayonnaise on top and more in a sauceboat on the side.

Suggested wine: Calloway Fumé Blanc.

Salads and Dressings

Aïoli Mayonnaise

Aïoli Mayonnaise

See Garlic Shrimp with Jalapeño Corn Bread (p. 31)
About 2 cups

9 cloves garlic
1½ cups mayonnaise
½ tablespoon (or more, to taste) lemon juice
½ teaspoon Dijon mustard
3 dashes Louisiana hot sauce
½ teaspoon Worcestershire sauce
¼ teaspoon sugar
pinch cayenne pepper

Blend the garlic, mayonnaise, and lemon juice in a blender until smooth, then combine with the rest.

Black-Eyed Pea Salad

Black-Eyed Pea Salad

About 2 cups

1 can whole black-eyed peas, drained and rinsed
1 tomato, seeded and chopped about the size of the peas
1 teaspoon lemon juice
1 jalapeño pepper, very finely chopped
¼ teaspoon cumin
½ clove (or more, to taste) garlic, finely chopped

3 tablespoons yogurt	lettuce, for beds
1 tablespoon cilantro,	lemon wedges, for garnish
finely chopped	cilantro sprigs, for garnish

Combine the ingredients and chill. Serve on lettuce leaves and garnish with lemon wedges and sprigs of cilantro.

Blue Cheese Dressing

About 6 cups

3 anchovy fillets	½ tablespoon dried tarragon
2 medium shallots	2 tablespoons tarragon vinegar
1–2 raw egg yolks*	¾ tablespoon Worcestershire
1 quart mayonnaise	sauce
½ cup Dijon mustard	1½ dashes Tabasco
¾ cup sour cream	¾ cup dried parsley
¼ tablespoon white pepper	¼ pound blue cheese,
½ tablespoon onion powder	crumbled

Blend the anchovy fillets, shallots, and egg yolks briefly in a blender. Pour into a bowl. Add the remaining ingredients. Mix thoroughly.

*An extra egg yolk may be added for richness, but the mayonnaise should not be too yellow.

Cantaloupe, Orange, and Red Onion Salad

4 servings

cantaloupe slices
orange sections
red onion, cut in half and sliced thin
lettuce leaves or watercress, for beds
¾ cup olive oil
¼ cup lime juice, freshly squeezed, of course!
1 tablespoon cilantro, chopped
ground black pepper, to taste
salt, to taste

Arrange the melon, orange, and onion slices attractively on salad plates on beds of lettuce or watercress. Combine the remaining ingredients and drizzle over the salad.

Caper Mayonnaise

Use this for shrimp cocktails.
2½ cups

1½ cups mayonnaise
1 raw egg yolk
2 tablespoons onion, chopped

¼ tablespoon dry mustard

1 tablespoon Dijon mustard

¾ cup capers

3 tablespoons lemon juice

Combine the ingredients.

Raw Mushroom Salad

Raw Mushroom Salad

4 servings

2 dozen medium mushrooms	¼ cup lime juice
½ teaspoon dry mustard	¼ cup parsley, chopped
½ teaspoon sugar	½ cup fresh dill weed,
2 teaspoons salt	chopped
½ teaspoon coarse pepper	lettuce leaves, for beds
1 clove garlic, crushed	chopped parsley, for garnish
1 cup olive oil	lime slices, for garnish

Wipe the mushrooms clean, trim the ends off the stems, and slice as thinly as possible. Mix gently with the remaining ingredients, and let stand for at least 30 minutes. Serve on beds of lettuce. Garnish with chopped parsley and slices of lime.

Cucumber Salad

Cucumber Salad

4 servings

2 tablespoons fresh mint, chopped

2 tablespoons cilantro, chopped

3 tablespoons sugar

1 tablespoon kosher salt

5 drops chili oil

½ teaspoon tumeric

⅛ teaspoon cumin

1 tablespoon fresh ginger, peeled and chopped

¼ cup lime juice

¼ cup rice vinegar

3 cucumbers, thinly sliced

lettuce leaves, for beds

chopped cilantro, for garnish

Combine the ingredients (cucumbers last). Chill for 1 hour. Serve on beds of lettuce and sprinkle with chopped cilantro.

Curried Mayonnaise

Curried Mayonnaise

See Chutney Eggs (p. 44).

About 3 cups

2 cups mayonnaise

1 tablespoon lime juice

¾–1 teaspoon curry powder

1 raw egg yolk

¾ cup parsley, chopped

½ teaspoon onion powder

¼ teaspoon dried ginger
dash Tabasco
dash Worcestershire sauce

Combine the ingredients.

Dill Mayonnaise

Almost 3 cups

2 cups mayonnaise
2 tablespoons fresh dill weed (or more, to taste)
1 raw egg yolk
2 tablespoons dill vinegar or white vinegar
1 tablespoon Dijon mustard
1 teaspoon onion powder
3 tablespoons lemon juice
few drops Tabasco

Combine the ingredients.

This is essential to the world-famous Trout Mousse (p. 98)

Garlic Vinaigrette

About 1½ cups

4 teaspoons Dijon mustard
6 tablespoons white wine vinegar
3 tablespoons hot water
1 tablespoon garlic, crushed
¾ cup olive oil
2 teaspoons onion powder
1 tablespoon sugar
1 teaspoon Worcestershire sauce
salt and pepper, to taste

Put the mustard and vinegar in a blender. On a low speed add the water and garlic, then slowly add the oil. Add the rest of the ingredients and mix well.

Green Goddess Dressing

About 7 cups

½ cup tarragon vinegar
2 tablespoons lemon juice
4 anchovy fillets
2 cloves garlic, crushed

3 raw egg yolks
4 cups mayonnaise
1 cup sour cream
¼ cup parsley, chopped

¼ cup fresh basil, chopped,	¼ cup chervil, chopped
or ⅛ cup dried basil	¼ cup chives, chopped
¼ cup fresh tarragon, chopped,	or freeze-dried
or ⅛ cup dried tarragon	

Put the vinegar, lemon juice, anchovies, garlic, and egg yolks in a blender and blend for 1 minute. Pour into a bowl, then add the remaining ingredients. It should not taste of mayonnaise.

Hot Tip: To give the dressing a pale green color, put some freshly chopped parsley in a towel and twist, letting the green liquid drip into the bowl.

Hot and Spicy Spinach Salad

2 cups

½ cup butter
½ cup cider vinegar
¼ cup Worcestershire sauce
⅓ cup catsup
½ cup sugar
spinach, rinsed, stems removed

Combine all but the spinach and bring to a boil and keep warm. Steam the spinach until it is hot and begins to wilt, then put in a bowl. Pour on the dressing, toss, and serve.

Hot Tip: The quickest way to prepare this salad is to toss everything together, including the spinach, then put it in a microwave on high for 20–30 seconds.

House Dressing
(A Vinaigrette)

About 6 cups

2 raw eggs*
1 quart vegetable oil
½ cup Dijon mustard
¼ cup lemon juice
¼ cup white vinegar
½ cup balsamic vinegar
½ tablespoon Worcestershire
   sauce
1 clove garlic, minced
1 ¼ tablespoons salt
½ tablespoon onion powder

¾ tablespoon ground black
   pepper
½ tablespoon white pepper
¾ tablespoon dry mustard
¼ tablespoon dried dill weed
2 tablespoons dried chervil
2 tablespoons dried basil
½ cup dried parsley
2 tablespoons freeze-dried
   chives
½ tablespoon sugar

Put the eggs in a food processor. With the machine on high slowly pour in the oil. Pour this mixture into a mixing bowl. Add the remaining ingredients and mix well.

*The eggs may be left out of this recipe, if desired. This may extend the storage life of the dressing.

**It's very helpful to put together several batches of the dry ingredients at the same time. Then, when you run out of dressing, just add the garlic and the liquids. Tom called these "Thank-Gods."

Lemon Dressing

Lemon Dressing

This dressing works well with the Melon, Orange, and Beet Salad
(p. 113).

About 2½ cups

2 cups olive oil
¼ cup lemon or lime juice, with grated rinds
¼ teaspoon salt
¼ teaspoon white pepper
¼ teaspoon sugar
1 dash Worcestershire sauce
1 tablespoon dry mustard
2 tablespoons fresh chives, chopped

Combine the ingredients.

Cauliflower Salad

Cauliflower Salad

1 serving

cauliflower flowerets
Roasted Red Bell Pepper Mayonnaise (p. 115)
Italian parsley, chopped

Parboil (see Swordfish on a Sword, p. 251) the flowerets just until tender. Plunge into ice water to stop cooking. Put some pepper mayonnaise on a salad plate, sprinkle with chopped parsley. Place the
flowerets on top, then more parsley.

Lobster Salad

Lobster Salad

8 servings

1 cup onions, finely chopped
½ cup green peppers,
   finely chopped
½ cup pimientos, finely chopped
1 cup celery, finely chopped
½ cup crisp bacon,
   finely chopped
½ cup Swiss cheese,
   finely chopped
3 anchovy fillets, finely chopped
⅓ cup capers, finely chopped
½ cup parsley, finely chopped
4 hard-boiled eggs, finely chopped
3 pounds cooked lobster meat,
   cut in bite-size pieces
mayonnaise
   (homemade, of course)
salt and pepper, to taste
lettuce leaves, for beds
32–40 asparagus spears,
   marinated in French dressing
lemon wedges, edges dipped in
   chopped basil
black and green olives,
   for garnish
chopped parsley, for garnish

Mix the first 10 ingredients in a bowl. Add the lobster, then bind it all together with mayonnaise. Taste for salt and pepper, then let stand for at least 30 minutes.

Put beds of lettuce on plates and arrange 4 or 5 asparagus spears as spokes toward the edges of the plates. Place some lobster salad in the middle. Put lemon wedges and black and green olives around the edges of the plates and between the spokes. Finish off each plate with 1 large wedge or crown of lemon in the middle and a sprinkle of chopped parsley. Serve with hot buttered toast or a loaf of hot garlic bread.

Melon, Orange, and Beet Salad

4 servings

8 slices ripe melon
24 slices cooked beet
24 slices orange
Boston lettuce leaves, for beds
1 cup olive oil
⅓ cup lemon juice
½ teaspoon sugar or honey
pinch white pepper
salt, to taste

On each plate layer 1 slice of melon, 3 beet slices, then 3 orange slices on beds of Boston lettuce and repeat to make an attractive pattern. Combine the remaining ingredients (or use Lemon Dressing, p. 111) and drizzle over the salad.

Pesto Vinaigrette

About 1¾ cups

½ cup virgin olive oil
½ cup vegetable oil
¼ cup balsamic vinegar
2 shallots, minced
1 clove garlic, minced
¼ teaspoon freshly ground
 black pepper

1 teaspoon salt
½ teaspoon sugar
2 tablespoons Pesto Sauce
 (p. 184)
3 tablespoons vinegar
3 tablespoons lemon juice

Combine the ingredients. Serve over the salad below.

Creole Tomato, Vidalia Onion, and Mozzarella Salad

creole tomatoes
Vidalia onions
mozzarella cheese
lettuce, for beds
chopped parsley or basil, for garnish

On beds of lettuce arrange layers of tomatoes, onions, and cheese.
Pour on the Pesto Vinaigrette just before serving, and sprinkle with
chopped parsley or basil.

Roasted Red Bell Pepper Mayonnaise

See Cauliflower Salad (p. 111)

About 3 cups

1 red bell pepper, finely chopped	1/8 cup white vinegar
olive oil, for rubbing peppers, plus 1 1/2 cups	1/2 teaspoon salt
	1/2 teaspoon white pepper
kosher salt	1 tablespoon red onion, chopped
2 raw egg yolks	1/4 teaspoon Dijon mustard
1/8 cup balsamic vinegar	1/2 teaspoon cayenne pepper

Cut the pepper in half and remove the seeds and membranes (one large pepper will yield about 1 cup chopped and roasted). Rub with olive oil and place cut side down on a sheet pan. Sprinkle with kosher salt. Put in a hot oven until the skin blisters and becomes crisp, but not blackened, keeping the red color for this recipe.

Put the egg yolks in a blender. Blend for 2 minutes, then slowly drizzle in 1½ cups of oil. Add the remaining ingredients. Blend well.

Smoked Eggplant Salad

Smoked Eggplant Salad

4 servings

2 eggplants, with the skin on	¼ teaspoon black pepper
olive oil	¼ teaspoon cinnamon
vegetable oil or clarified butter	(optional)
(see Barbecued Shrimp,	dash cayenne pepper
p. 39) for sautéing	2 tablespoons fresh mint,
2 cloves garlic, minced	chopped
¾ cup onions, minced	1 tablespoon cilantro,
1 jalapeño pepper, minced	chopped
3 tomatoes, peeled (see	1½ cups plain yogurt
Eggplant Provençal, p. 60),	cilantro sprigs, for garnish
seeded, and chopped	toasties, for garnish (see Chef's
1 teaspoon ground cumin	Yeast Rolls, p. 30)

Cut the eggplants into halves and rub with olive oil. Grill over charcoal or bake in the oven until tender. Cool, then squeeze out as much of the moisture as possible. Chop the eggplant and put into a bowl. Sauté the garlic, onions, and jalapeño pepper in vegetable oil or clarified butter until tender. Add the tomatoes, cumin, pepper, cinnamon, and cayenne. Combine with the eggplant. Add the mint, chopped cilantro, and yogurt and chill well. Garnish with sprigs of cilantro and toasties.

Summer Garden Salad

6 servings

4 ripe tomatoes, seeded and
  coarsely chopped
½ cup red onions, chopped
1 cup red bell peppers, chopped
1 clove garlic, finely chopped
1½ cups cucumbers, peeled,
  seeded, and chopped
6 radishes, sliced,
  then cut in halves
3 tablespoons fresh basil,
  very finely chopped

½ cup plain yogurt
3 tablespoons lemon juice
½ teaspoon salt
½ teaspoon white pepper
¼ cup catsup or ½ teaspoon
  tomato paste, mixed with
1 teaspoon sugar
lettuce leaves
rye toast or toasties (see Chef's
  Yeast Rolls, p. 30),
  accompaniment

Put the vegetables and basil into a bowl. Chill well. Make a lemon yogurt dressing by combining the remaining ingredients. Put the salad in a leaf-lined bowl or on lettuce leaves on salad plates. Pass the dressing. Serve with thin slices of rye toast or toasties.

Tomato Salad Dressing

Tomato Salad Dressing

About 4 cups

2 cups scallions, white and green parts, finely chopped,
   or 2 cups freeze-dried chives
2½ cups white vinegar
1 large clove garlic, minced
½ cup parsley, chopped
¼ cup olive oil
1½ tablespoons salt
4 tablespoons sugar
½ teaspoon crushed black pepper

Combine the ingredients. Serve over the salad below.

T. C.'s Tomato Salad

Boston or Bibb lettuce
tomato slices
onion slices
parsley, chopped, for garnish

On a bed of Boston or Bibb lettuce place slices of tomato with alternating layers of sliced onion. Pour the dressing on just before serving. Garnish with freshly chopped parsley.

Watercress, Bacon, and Mushroom Salad

4 servings

1 bunch watercress, washed, stems removed

1 stale end piece of bread

1 whole clove garlic

½ teaspoon salt

½ teaspoon dry mustard

½ teaspoon black pepper

1 teaspoon onion powder

½ teaspoon sugar

1 teaspoon Dijon mustard

6 tablespoons olive oil

2 tablespoons white or red wine vinegar

dash Worcestershire sauce

½ pound sliced mushrooms, tossed in lemon juice

8 slices crisp bacon, finely chopped

4–8 hard-boiled egg yolks, sieved (optional)

cherry tomatoes, halved, for garnish

Pat the watercress dry and refrigerate in a towel. Rub the piece of bread with the clove of garlic, then put the bread in the bottom of a wooden salad bowl. Add the spices, sugar, mustard, oil, vinegar, and Worcestershire sauce and stir well. When ready to serve, remove the piece of bread, and toss the watercress and mushrooms in the dressing. Put on chilled plates, sprinkle with the chopped bacon and sieved egg yolks, and garnish with halves of cherry tomatoes.

Soups

Tom wrote, "Of all the aspects of cooking, I personally feel that the making of a soup can be the most rewarding. There is something so reassuring about a pot simmering away, chock-full of good things and getting better by the moment.

"True, there is not the instant gratification of removing a finished dish from the oven. But there is the great reward of tasting and savoring the final blend of herbs, vegetables, chicken, or meats that can't really be matched, and then saying, 'I did that myself!'"

Bean and Bacon Soup

Bean and Bacon Soup

6–8 servings

1 pound (about 2 cups) white navy beans	2½ cups tomatoes, peeled (see Eggplant Provençal, p. 60), seeded, and chopped
1 pound bacon, cut in small squares	½ teaspoon coarse black pepper
1 cup celery, finely chopped	1 quart Beef Stock (p. 22)
2 cups onions, finely chopped	2 whole bay leaves (remove before serving)
½ cup carrots, finely chopped	chopped parsley, for garnish
3 cloves garlic, chopped	chopped bacon, for garnish

Wash the beans and let soak overnight, if possible. Remove any float-ing beans. Strain, saving 1 quart or so of the bean water.

Put the bacon in a 3-quart pot and cook until crisp. Remove the bacon, pour off most of the fat, then add the celery, onions, carrots, garlic, tomatoes, and black pepper. Cook for 5 minutes. Add the beans, bean water, most of the cooked bacon (saving some for garnish-ing later), Beef Stock, and bay leaves. Simmer until the beans are soft, about 4 hours. Thin, if necessary, with Beef Stock. If the soup is too thin, remove and blend some of the beans, then return them to the pot. Serve sprinkled with chopped parsley and chopped bacon.

Black Bean Soup

10–12 servings

1 pound (2 cups) black beans	pinch powdered thyme
½ pound salt pork, cut into tiny squares	1–1½ cups cooking sherry
2 cups onions, finely chopped	1 lemon
1 cup celery, finely chopped	8 cloves
2 cloves garlic, finely chopped	¼ pound sweet butter
1 cup carrots, finely chopped	circular slices of lemon or lime, for garnish
½ teaspoon black pepper	hard-boiled egg yolks, for garnish
1 tablespoon tomato paste	chopped parsley, for garnish
4 dashes Tabasco	good sherry
2–3 quarts Beef Stock (p. 22)	red peppercorns
1 soup bone, if available	
2 whole bay leaves	

Wash the beans and soak overnight, if possible. Remove any floating beans, strain, and set aside.

Brown the salt pork in a soup kettle. Remove the pork and pour off most of the fat. Add the vegetables, garlic, black pepper, tomato paste, and Tabasco to the pot and cook for 10 minutes, stirring often. Add the beans and cover with Beef Stock, plus 1 extra quart. Add the soup bone, bay leaves, thyme, ½–1 cup (to your taste) sherry, and the lemon stuck with the cloves.

Simmer until the beans are soft (about 3 hours), stirring often so the pot doesn't scorch. Discard the lemon, bay leaves, and soup bone. Blend the soup in a blender and strain into the top of a double boiler. If the soup is too thick, thin with Beef Stock and/or sherry. Heat for another 30 minutes or until serving time. Add the sweet butter and taste for salt.

To serve, put the soup in warm bowls and float circles of seeded lemon or lime decorated with small amounts of sieved hard-boiled egg yolk and chopped parsley. Pass a cruet of good sherry in which, if you wish, several red peppercorns have been soaking.

Black Mushroom Soup

8–10 servings

2 quarts rich Chicken Stock (p. 24) or a simple stock made with:	chicken necks or a whole chicken
4 quarts water	1 ½ pounds mushrooms, finely chopped (stems are okay)
12 chicken bouillon cubes	1 cup cooking sherry
1 large onion, quartered	1 cup beef bouillon
2 carrots, quartered	salt and pepper, to taste
celery tops	whipped cream
1 whole bay leaf	chives or nutmeg, for garnish

Heat 2 quarts of rich Chicken Stock, or make a simple stock by heating the water, bouillon cubes, onion, carrots, celery, bay leaf, and chicken. Simmer until the chicken is tender, about 20–30 minutes. Remove the chicken (save for other dishes). Strain the rich stock and reduce by cooking to 2 quarts.

Put the mushrooms, sherry, and bouillon in a 4-quart pot. Cook for 15 minutes, then add the hot rich stock. Simmer for at least 1 hour. Then taste for salt and pepper.

Put into individual soup crocks and top with unsweetened whipped cream, which can be browned under the broiler. Sprinkle with chopped chives or a tiny dash of nutmeg.

Chicken Consommé

Chicken Consommé

The Chicken Stock for these recipes should be extra rich.

6 servings

Variation 1

1 quart Chicken Stock (p. 24)
½ bottle good dry white wine or flat champagne
1 truffle, cooked in sherry (optional)

Bring the Chicken Stock to a simmer. Add the wine or champagne. Simmer for 20 minutes. Serve in 6 consommé cups in its pale golden purity. Or, if you are feeling (or you are) very rich and have a truffle within reach, cook it in a little sherry, cut it into little diamonds, then add it to the consommé.

Variation 2

1 quart Chicken Stock (p. 24)
2–3 cups good dry sherry
6 teaspoons chicken, cubed small
salted whipped cream, for garnish

Bring the Chicken Stock to a simmer. Add the sherry. Simmer for 20 minutes. Put the chicken in the bottom of 6 consommé cups. Pour in the very hot soup. Garnish with whipped cream to which a pinch of salt has been added.

Cock-a-Leekie

8 servings

1½ quarts Chicken Stock (p. 24)	2 pieces raw bacon, cut in small pieces
3 potatoes, cut in small cubes	1 rib celery, diced small
8 small leeks, thoroughly cleaned, cut in 1-inch strips	1 cup boiled chicken, finely cubed
1 small carrot, thinly sliced	chopped parsley, for garnish

Put everything but the chicken in a 3-quart pot. Cook until the vegetables are soft, about 10 minutes, then add the chicken. Serve immediately with sprinkles of chopped parsley.

The 1974 staff picture from Tom Cowman's Restaurant

Chicken Gumbo

10–12 servings

2 quarts Chicken Stock (p. 24)
1 small boiling chicken, plus any
   extra necks or bones
1 veal knuckle, cracked,
   if available
3 onions, quartered
2 carrots, quartered
5 whole cloves garlic
2 whole bay leaves
10 black peppercorns
4 strips bacon, cut in small
   pieces
1 ½ cups onions, finely chopped
1 ½ cups green peppers,
   diced small
¼ cup celery, finely chopped
½ carrot, finely chopped

6 tomatoes, peeled (see
   Eggplant Provençal, p. 60),
   seeded, and chopped
1 cup ham, cubed small
⅓ cup uncooked rice
12 or more okra, cut in circles
   (frozen okra is okay)
2 cups mustard greens,
   finely chopped
1 tablespoon gumbo filé powder
1 cup cooking sherry
4–5 dashes Tabasco
2 cups chicken, cut into squares
cooked rice, accompaniment
chopped parsley, for garnish

Put the stock, small boiling chicken, bones, veal knuckle, the quartered onions and carrots, garlic, bay leaves, and peppercorns in a 6-quart pot or soup kettle. Cook until the chicken is tender, about 20–30 minutes. Remove the chicken, clean the meat (save it for later) from the bones, then return the bones to the pot.

Cook 1 more hour, then strain. Cook the bacon in the same pot. When done, remove the bacon and pour off most of the fat. Add the chopped onions, peppers, celery, chopped carrot, tomatoes, ham, and bacon to the pot and cook for 5 minutes, stirring often. Pour in the strained stock and bring to a boil. When the soup begins to boil, reduce to a simmer and add the rice, okra, greens, and filé powder. Cook very slowly (don't boil—the filé powder will get stringy) for about 45 minutes, stirring often so it doesn't stick or scorch. Add the sherry, Tabasco, and 2 cups of chicken and cook 15 minutes. Serve with rice and garnish with chopped parsley.

Clam Bisque

This soup was the most popular one served at Gordon's Restaurant. It was a permanent fixture on the menu.

6 servings

2 cups Cream Soup Base
   (p. 131)
1 cup chopped fresh clams,
   with the juice, or 1 cup
   canned minced clams
½ cup heavy cream

1 cup Half & Half
2 tablespoons sweet butter
salt and white pepper, to taste
6 butter pats
paprika or cayenne pepper,
   for color

Heat the Cream Soup Base in the top of a double boiler. Put the clams and clam juice in a blender and blend well. Add to the soup base. Heat gently. Thin to the proper consistency (fairly thick and creamy, not watery) by whisking in the heavy cream and Half & Half. Add the sweet butter. Taste for salt and white pepper. Serve in individual bowls or cups. Float a pat of butter on top. Sprinkle lightly with paprika or cayenne pepper.

Corn Bisque

8 servings

3 fifteen-ounce cans creamed corn

3 tablespoons butter

3 tablespoons Seasoned Flour (p. 27)

4 chicken bouillon cubes, dissolved in a little water

2 cups heavy cream

2 cups Half & Half

few dashes of Louisiana hot sauce or Tabasco

1 tablespoon white wine Worcestershire sauce

3 tablespoons Maître d'Hôtel Butter (p. 26)

1 cup cubed Jalapeño Corn Bread, toasted (p. 31)

Blend the creamed corn well (thinning with a little water if the blender clogs up), then strain. Make a white roux by melting the butter in a heavy, 3-quart pot, adding the flour, and cooking for 5 minutes, stirring constantly and making sure it doesn't turn brown. Add the strained corn, whisking until the flour taste is gone and the soup is thickened. Add the bouillon cubes, cream, and Half & Half. Add the hot sauce and Worcestershire and taste for salt. Cook without boiling for 10 minutes or more, stirring.

Just before serving add the Maître d'Hôtel Butter. Garnish with a few small cubes of toasted Jalapeño Corn Bread.

This is wonderful with lump crabmeat, shrimp, or crawfish added at the last moment. (If you plan on doing this, substitute fish broth and cubes for the chicken broth and cubes.)

Cream Soup Base

Cream Soup Base

This soup base can be used for vichyssoise and most cream of vegetable, chicken, or seafood soups. It can be frozen.

About 6 cups

2 potatoes, peeled and diced
2 leeks, white part only, washed and quartered
2 ribs celery, chopped
1 small onion, chopped
1 carrot, cut in half
2 whole bay leaves
1 piece bacon
2–3 cups rich Chicken Stock (p. 24) or
   seafood stock (see Fish Stock, p. 25)

Put everything in a heavy, 3-quart pot. Bring to a boil. Cook until the vegetables are soft, about 20 minutes. Remove from the fire and let cool. Remove the bay leaves and one piece of carrot. Blend until smooth and strain. Use immediately or cool well before refrigerating or freezing.

Vegetables that can be used with this base include (but are not limited to) asparagus, broccoli, carrots, cauliflower, roasted red bell peppers, summer squash, watercress, and zucchini.

Cream of Chicken Soup

Cream of Chicken Soup

8 servings

3 cups Cream Soup Base (p. 131)
2 cups rich Chicken Stock (p. 24)
4 raw egg yolks, separate
1 cup (or more) heavy cream
¼ cup grated Parmesan cheese
pinch powdered thyme
small pinch nutmeg (optional)
1½ cups cooked chicken, cut in small squares
salt and pepper, to taste
paprika, for color

Heat the base and stock in the top of a double boiler. When hot, whip in the egg yolks one at a time and beat for 5–6 minutes or until the mixture is thick and creamy. Add cream until the desired texture is reached. Whip in the cheese, thyme, and nutmeg. Add the cooked chicken and taste for seasonings, salt, and pepper. Serve with sprinkles of paprika.

Cream of Scallop Soup

4–6 servings

2 cups Cream Soup Base (p. 131)
1 cup Half & Half
1 cup cream
1 pint bay scallops
salt and white pepper, to taste
4–6 sweet butter pats
cayenne pepper, for color

Heat the base, cream, and Half & Half in a double boiler. When it's very hot, add the scallops and cook for 10 minutes. Do not overcook as the scallops will become tough. Taste for salt and white pepper. Serve in soup cups topped with pats of sweet butter and a light dusting of cayenne pepper.

Cream of Avocado Soup

Cream of Avocado Soup

4–6 servings

2 cups Cream Soup Base (p. 131)
1 cup heavy cream
1 cup Half & Half
2 avocados, mashed or blended
pinch nutmeg
salt and white pepper, to taste
sour cream, for garnish
chives, chopped, for garnish
avocado, cut in squares, for garnish
lime juice, for garnish
parsley, for color (optional)

Heat the base, cream, and Half & Half in a double boiler. (If this is to be served cold, the soup need not be heated. Just whip the ingredients together and garnish as below.) Add the avocados and nutmeg, and taste for salt and pepper. Garnish with dollops of sour cream, sprinkles of chopped chives, and little squares of avocado that have been tossed in lime juice. If a greener color is desired, put some parsley in a clean towel, then wring the towel until the green liquid drips into the soup.

Fish Chowder

8–10 servings

¼ cup salt pork, finely minced
¾ cup onions, diced
½ cup celery, diced
½ cup carrots, diced
2½ cups canned peeled
   tomatoes or 4–5 whole
   tomatoes, peeled (see
   Eggplant Provençal, p. 60),
   seeded, and chopped
1 eleven-and-one-half-ounce
   bottle clamato juice
1 eleven-and-one-half-ounce
   bottle tomato juice

4 fish bouillon cubes
1 whole bay leaf
¼ teaspoon powdered thyme
1 tablespoon freeze-dried
   chives
1 tablespoon parsley, chopped
1 cup potatoes, diced
2 cups blackfish, flounder,
   or any non-oily fish, diced
salt and pepper, to taste

Cook the salt pork in a 3-quart pot over medium heat until brown.
Remove the pork and drain off most of the fat. Add the onions, celery,
and carrots and cook until almost tender, about 5–6 minutes. Add the
rest of the ingredients, except the fish, salt, and pepper. Cook until the
potatoes are almost soft, about 20 minutes. Add the fish and cook for 5
minutes. Remove from the fire. Taste for seasonings.

Fresh Pea or Lima Bean Soup

8–10 servings

½ cup butter
½ cup onions, finely chopped
½ slice bacon
1 ½ quarts Chicken Stock (p. 24)
3 cups shelled fresh peas or lima beans
1 tablespoon all-purpose flour, blended with
1 tablespoon soft butter
salt and pepper, to taste

Melt the butter in a 3-quart pot. Add the onions and bacon and cook for 5 minutes. Add the stock and peas or lima beans, and bring to a simmer. Cook until the vegetables are soft, about 20 minutes. Thicken with the blended flour and butter. Taste for salt and pepper.

Fresh Tomato Soup

Tom wrote, "This is wonderful when tomatoes are plentiful and vine ripened."

8 servings

¼ cup sweet butter
¼ cup onion, chopped
½ clove garlic, crushed
½ cup celery, chopped
1 tablespoon sugar
8 large tomatoes, peeled (see
  Eggplant Provençal, p. 60),
  seeded, and chopped
1 teaspoon salt

¼ teaspoon white pepper
½ quart Chicken Stock (p. 24)
1 whole bay leaf
2 tomatoes, peeled, seeded,
  and sliced into thin strips
1 cup cream, salted and
  whipped
¼ cup fresh basil or dill,
  chopped

Melt the sweet butter in a 3-quart soup pot. Add the onions, garlic, and celery and cook for 3 minutes. Add the remaining ingredients, except the tomato strips, cream, and basil or dill, and cook for 30 minutes. Blend well in a blender, return to the pot, and taste for salt and pepper. Just before serving add the tomato strips. Serve with dollops of slightly salted, whipped cream that has been mixed with chopped fresh basil or dill.

This is delicious cold too. Chill before adding the fresh tomato strips. Garnish with orange slices.

Garlic Vichyssoise

8 servings

> 2–3 whole heads garlic
> 1 quart Chicken Stock (p. 24)
> 4 potatoes, peeled and quartered
> ¾ cup celery, chopped
> 1 carrot, chopped
> 1 cup onions, chopped
> 1 cup Half & Half
> 1 cup (or more) heavy cream
> chopped garlic chives, for garnish

Put the garlic and stock in a 2-quart pot and bring to a simmer. Remove the garlic when it's soft, about 15 minutes. Add the vegetables and cook over medium heat until they are tender, about 10 minutes. Cool, then blend well. Taste for garlic flavor. If it's not strong enough, blend in peeled cloves of cooked garlic until the flavor is how you like it. Add Half & Half and cream until thick and creamy. Chill well. Serve in chilled bowls, garnished with chopped garlic chives.

The Buxton Inn, Guanville, Ohio

Gazpacho

Tom wrote, "This is, without doubt, one of the great soups. It takes time to make as the vegetables have to be carefully prepared. No blenders! It is a completely individual soup. Some prefer less oil, more cucumber, less green pepper, and so forth, so the amounts given are meant as guides."

8 servings

¼ cup green peppers, diced

¼ cup sweet red peppers, diced

½ cup celery, diced

½ cup scallions with tops, diced

½ cup cucumbers, seeded, soaked in iced salt water, and diced

¼ clove garlic, very finely minced

¼ cup parsley, minced

¼ cup fresh basil, minced

4 tomatoes, peeled (see Eggplant Provençal, p. 60), seeded, and chopped

1 cup good olive oil

1 cup tomato juice

¼ cup vinegar

¼ teaspoon (or more) coarse black pepper

salt, to taste

Dice the vegetables to the size of a kitchen matchhead. Combine the oil, tomato juice, and vinegar in a stainless steel bowl or earthen crock that is set down in bowl of ice. Stir in the vegetables and herbs, then add the salt and pepper. Serve as cold as possible with hot, buttered toast.

Tom wrote, "A friend in Spain keeps a large jug of this handy for the morning to add to, some say, a little vodka."

Iced Cream of Watercress Soup

6 servings

2 bunches watercress, big stems removed
½ cup Chicken Stock (p. 24)
2 cups Cream Soup Base (p. 131)
2 cups heavy cream
1 cup (or more) Half & Half
1 good dash cayenne pepper
salt and white pepper, to taste

Cook the watercress in a little Chicken Stock for about 2 minutes, or until wilted. Cool, then blend well, using more of the Chicken Stock. Mix the blended watercress into the Cream Soup Base. Add the remaining ingredients. Mix well, thinning with more Half & Half if it's too thick. Taste for salt & white pepper and refrigerate until very cold. Serve in chilled soup cups.

Italian Romaine Soup

1 serving

romaine lettuce, shredded
1 cup (or more) rich Chicken Stock (p. 24)
grated Romano cheese, on the side

Wash the lettuce, remove the coarse fibers, cut into shreds, and put into bowls full of very hot rich Chicken Stock. Serve immediately with freshly grated Romano cheese on the side.

Jellied Madrilène à la Russe

12 servings

1½ quarts rich Beef Stock (p. 22)	1 cup cooking sherry
4 ribs celery, quartered	red food coloring (optional)
2 onions, quartered	sour cream, for garnish
6 cloves	red caviar, for garnish
3 whole cloves garlic	(Variation 1)
1 quart tomato juice	chives, chopped, for garnish
2 cups dry white wine	(Variation 2)
3 whole bay leaves	basil, for garnish (Variation 2)
4 tablespoons unsweetened gelatin	lime slices, for garnish (Variation 2)

Put the first 8 ingredients in a 3-quart pot and cook until the vegetables are tender. Strain through cheesecloth or a fine wire sieve. Return the broth to the kettle and clarify (see Beef Stock, p. 22). Add the gelatin mixed with sherry. If the color is not red enough, add a little red food coloring. Pour into a bowl and allow to chill and firm. To serve, cut into chunks with 2 knives. Put into chilled consommé bowls. Garnish with good dollops of sour cream topped with good red caviar. Another way to garnish this is with sour cream mixed with chopped fresh chives and basil, then topped with lime slices.

Gumbo Z'Herbes

Gumbo Z'Herbes

About 12 servings

2 tablespoons garlic, chopped

¾ cup onions, chopped

½ cup green peppers, chopped

butter, for sautéing

1 cup mustard greens,
stems removed, chopped

1 cup collard greens,
stems removed, chopped

1 cup turnip greens, stems
removed, chopped

¼ cup watercress, stems
removed, chopped

¼ cup parsley, stems removed,
chopped

½ cup spinach, stems removed,
chopped

¾ cup scallions, green and
white parts, chopped

½ small cabbage,
finely chopped

1 cup celery leaves, chopped

2 quarts (or more) Chicken
Stock (p. 24)

2 cups canned beef broth

⅛ teaspoon black pepper

1 jalapeño pepper,
finely chopped

1 whole bay leaf

½ tablespoon gumbo filé
powder

white pepper or Louisiana
hot sauce, to taste

In a 5-quart pot briefly sauté the garlic, onions, and peppers in a little butter. Add everything but the filé powder and white pepper or hot sauce and cook slowly for 1 hour. Add more stock to cover, if necessary. Take out half of the greens, process briefly (don't puree, just make smaller), return to the pot, and cook another 30 minutes. Add the filé powder and continue to simmer. Do not boil. Taste for white pepper or hot sauce.

Lentil Soup

As with most soups, this gets better after standing for a day.

8–10 servings

1 pound (2 cups) lentils	4 dashes Tabasco
½ pound salt pork, cubed small	ham bone, ham scraps, ham
1 cup onions, finely chopped	hock, or lamb shanks,
1 cup celery, finely chopped	browned in oil
1 cup carrots, finely chopped	salt and pepper, to taste
3 cloves garlic	8 garlic frankfurters, sliced
3 whole bay leaves	½ cup parsley, chopped
2½ cups Italian tomatoes	
1½ quarts Chicken (p. 24)	
or Beef Stock (p. 22)	

Soak the lentils overnight, remove any that float, and check for possible stones. Cook the salt pork in a 3-quart pot. Remove when browned and pour off most of the fat. Add the onions, celery, carrots, garlic, and bay leaves. Cook for 10 minutes, stirring until the vegetables are browned. Add the tomatoes, stock, Tabasco, lentils, and bone. Cook slowly until the lentils are soft, about 2 hours. Taste for salt and pepper. Five minutes before serving, remove the bay leaves. Stir in the frankfurters and most of the parsley. Serve with additional sprinkles of chopped parsley.

Lobster Bisque
à la Venezuela

8–10 servings

2 cups Cream Soup Base (p. 131)

1 can beef consommé

1 can pea soup

1 can tomato soup

1 tablespoon paprika

1 cup (more or less, to your taste) cooking sherry

1 cup (or more) cream

1 two-pound lobster, boiled or steamed, then cooled

salt, to taste

½ cup whipped cream, for garnish

cayenne pepper, for garnish

Combine the base, soups, and paprika in a double boiler. Add sherry and cream until the soup is thick and creamy. Remove the coral (the red roe), tomalley (the green liver), and meat from the lobster, and cut into small chunks. Stir these into the soup. Taste for sherry and salt. Serve with good dollops of unsweetened, whipped cream and small sprinkles of cayenne pepper.

Minestrone

Of this Tom wrote, "This is a hodgepodge and I love it!"

About 10 servings

1½ quarts Beef Stock (p. 22)

½ cup green beans, cut up

½ cup peas

½ cup onions, chopped

½ cup chick peas

½ cup white beans and/or
   kidney beans

½ cup celery, chopped

½ cup carrots, chopped

¼ cup uncooked rice
   (or ½ cup cooked rice)
   or ½ cup vermicelli
   (or other uncooked pasta)

4 cloves garlic, chopped

2 cups tomatoes, peeled (see
   Eggplant Provençal, p. 60),
   seeded, and chopped

1 cup fresh spinach or lettuce,
   chopped

¼ cup basil, chopped

¼ cup parsley, chopped

1 cup ham or bacon, chopped

salt and pepper, to taste

parsley, chopped, for garnish

grated Parmesan cheese,
   on the side

Put everything in a 3-quart pot or large soup kettle. In short, put whatever you have, preferably fresh vegetables. Cook until the vegetables are tender. Taste for salt and pepper. Serve with a sprinkle of chopped parsley and a dish of freshly grated Parmesan cheese on the side.

Mushroom Soup Supreme

Mushroom Soup Supreme

"Simple?" Tom wrote. "Yes, but just taste it!"
8 servings

> 1 ½ quarts Chicken Stock (p. 24)
> 3 cups mushrooms, finely chopped
> 1 cup cooking sherry
> salt and pepper, to taste
> ½ cup whipped cream, for garnish

Put the stock and mushrooms in a 3-quart soup pot and cook for 45 minutes. Add the sherry, cook for 15 minutes, and taste for seasoning. Serve in warmed consommé cups, topping each with a spoonful of unsweetened, whipped cream.

Garlic Soup

Garlic Soup

8 servings

> 1 ½ quarts rich Chicken Stock (p. 24)
> 12–18 cloves garlic, crushed
> 8 tablespoons lightly beaten egg or 8 whole raw quail eggs
> chopped parsley, for garnish

Put the stock and garlic in a 2-quart pot. Simmer for 1 hour, then strain. Return to the stove and bring to a boil. Pour the boiling soup into consommé cups. Drop in the raw eggs and garnish with chopped parsley.

Mussel Soup Amagansett

8 servings

¼ cup salt pork, cut in cubes

1 cup onions, finely chopped

4 cloves garlic, finely chopped

½ cup celery, finely chopped

¼ cup carrots, finely chopped

2 cups tomatoes, peeled (see
   Eggplant Provençal, p. 60),
   seeded, and chopped

2 cups tomato juice

½ cup basil, chopped

¼ cup parsley, chopped

2 cups dry white wine

4 whole bay leaves

48 mussels, cleaned (see
   Mussels in Garlic Sauce,
   p. 76)

chopped parsley, for garnish

Brown the salt pork in a soup pot over medium heat. Remove the pork and pour off most of the fat. Add everything except the mussels. Cook until the vegetables are browned and tender, about 10 minutes, then remove the bay leaves. Add the mussels. Serve in soup bowls as soon as the mussels open. Garnish with chopped parsley.

The staff of Gordon's Restaurant, Amagansett, Long Island, 1965

Navy Bean Soup

12 servings

1 pound (2 cups) navy beans	1 cup (or less, to taste) cooking
½ pound salt pork, cut into	sherry
small cubes	1 ham bone, hock, or ham
2 cups onions, finely chopped	scraps, finely chopped
1 cup celery, finely chopped	1 quart (or more) Chicken
1 small carrot, finely chopped	Stock (p. 24)
2 cloves garlic, crushed	a little salt
2 whole bay leaves	½ teaspoon white pepper
6 cloves	chopped ham, for garnish
4 dashes Tabasco	chopped parsley, for garnish
pinch powdered thyme	

Wash the beans, then soak overnight. Drain, saving 1 quart of the bean water.

In a soup kettle fry the salt pork until light brown. Remove and drain off most of the fat. To the fat add the vegetables, bay leaves, cloves, Tabasco, and thyme. Cook until the vegetables are transparent but not brown, about 5–6 minutes. Add the beans, bean water, cooked salt pork, sherry, and the ham bone, hock, or scraps. Cover with Chicken Stock and add the salt and white pepper. Cook slowly until the beans are soft, an hour or more.

If the soup is too thick, thin with Chicken Stock. If it's too thin, remove and blend some of the beans, then return them to the pot. Just before serving taste for salt and seasonings. Serve with a little chopped ham in the bottom of each bowl and top with generous sprinkles of chopped parsley.

Tabasco and a cruet of sherry vinegar may be passed at the table.

Oaxaca Lime Soup

6–8 servings

2 quarts rich Chicken Stock
   (p. 24) or a simple stock
made from:
  1 two-to three-pound
    chicken, cut up
  1 large onion with skin,
    quartered
  3 cloves garlic
  2 carrots, quartered
  2 whole bay leaves
  2 celery ribs with tops,
    quartered
  2 large parsley sprigs

6–8 chicken bouillon cubes,
    dissolved in 1 gallon water
1 cup fresh spinach,
  cut in small strips
1 cup radishes, thinly sliced
1 cup mushrooms, thinly sliced
1 cup avocado, chopped
1 cup scallions, chopped
1 cup boiled chicken, diced
1 cup lime juice
toasted tortilla strips,
  for garnish
lime, for garnish

Heat or make the stock. Or make the simple stock (see Chicken
Stock, p. 24) and reduce by half by boiling. Put about 1 tablespoon of
each ingredient in the bottom of each bowl. Pour in the boiling
Chicken Stock. Sprinkle in some tortilla strips and float lime slices on
top. Serve with lime wedges.

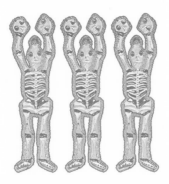

Onion Soup

This is better for lunch or a late supper. It's a bit heavy for a soup course.

6 servings

> 1 cup sweet butter
> 8 medium to large onions, thinly sliced
> 1 teaspoon sugar (optional)
> 2 quarts Beef Stock (p. 22)
> 6 slices French bread, toasted
> grated Parmesan cheese, on the side
> Swiss or Gruyère cheese (optional)

Melt the butter in a 3-quart soup pot, then add the onions and cook slowly until golden brown. (A teaspoon of sugar may be added to aid browning.) When brown, cover with the stock, and cook for at least 1 hour.

Serve in soup bowls with a slice of toasted French bread in each. Pass a dish of freshly grated Parmesan cheese. If you wish, the soup may be put into French onion soup crocks with the slices of French bread, topped with grated Swiss or Gruyère cheese along with the grated Parmesan, then put into a hot oven or under the broiler until the cheese melts and bubbles.

Oyster, Artichoke, and Mushroom Soup

8 servings

3 pints oysters, with their liquor
2 whole cloves garlic
1 teaspoon white pepper
1 teaspoon black pepper
1 teaspoon cayenne pepper
1 teaspoon sage
1 teaspoon leaf thyme
1 teaspoon oregano
1 teaspoon basil
¼ cup butter

1 pound fresh mushrooms, finely chopped
6 tablespoons all-purpose flour
1 cup rich Chicken Stock (p. 24)
2 fifteen-ounce cans artichoke bottoms,* drained and quartered
1 quart heavy cream

Put 2 pints of the oysters (with their liquor) into a heavy, 3-quart pot over medium heat. Blend the rest of the oysters and the garlic until smooth, then add to the pot. Add the seasonings and cook for 10–12 minutes.

Meanwhile, melt the butter in a saucepan. Add the mushrooms and sauté briefly. When they begin to soften, sprinkle in the flour. Cook for another 5 minutes. Add the stock a little at a time, stirring briskly, until all of it is incorporated. The mixture should be thick. Let the mixture cool slightly. Add it a little at a time to the oyster mixture, stirring briskly. Let this cook for approximately 20 minutes, stirring often. Add the artichoke bottoms and cream. Heat for 10–15 minutes more, until it's heated through. Taste for salt.

*Use bottoms that are packed in water, not the marinated kind. Of course, the hearts from your own freshly cooked artichokes (see Hot or Cold Artichokes, p. 68) would be marvelous. A lot of work, perhaps, but then again . . .

Oysters Rockefeller Soup

8 servings

2 tablespoons butter

1 cup celery, finely chopped

1 cup onions, finely chopped

2 cloves garlic, finely chopped

2 tablespoons all-purpose flour

2 quarts oyster liquid or
   clam juice

2 dozen oysters (sans pearls!)

½ pound spinach, no stems

1 bunch watercress, no stems

1 cup parsley, no stems

1 cup celery tops,
   coarsely chopped

1 cup heavy cream

2 tablespoons Pernod or
   Herbsaint

5 dashes Tabasco

1 teaspoon onion powder

1 tablespoon capers, blended

1 cup whipped cream, for garnish

Melt the butter in a 3-quart pot. Add the celery, onions, and garlic. Cook over medium heat until tender, about 5 minutes. Dissolve the flour in a little oyster liquid or clam juice. Add to the pot and cook for a few minutes. Add the remaining oyster liquid or clam juice. Blend the oysters briefly in a blender. Add to the liquid. Cook for 10 minutes. Briefly boil or steam the spinach, watercress, parsley, and celery tops, just until they wilt. Blend briefly in the blender. Add to the pot of liquid. Bring to a simmer. Add the remaining ingredients, except the whipped cream. Let simmer, adding water or oyster juice if it gets too thick. Don't overcook or the vegetables will lose their color. Serve with dabs of unsweetened, whipped cream, browning the top of the cream under the broiler for a brief moment.

Portuguese Fish Soup

8 servings

2 tablespoons salt pork,
  finely diced
¼ cup butter
2 cups onions, finely chopped
1 cup celery, finely chopped
1 carrot, finely chopped
1 quart rich Fish Stock (p. 25)
10 threads saffron
1 quart Half & Half
2 tablespoons Maître d'Hôtel
  Butter (p. 26)

2 large potatoes,
  peeled and diced
2 cups cubed firm fish, shrimp,
  and/or crabmeat
1 cup dry white wine,
  for poaching
cayenne pepper or paprika,
  for color

Cook the salt pork in a heavy, 4-quart saucepan over medium heat. When brown, add the butter. When the butter is hot, add the onions, celery, and carrot. Cook for 2–3 minutes, stirring, then add the stock. Cook, stirring, until the vegetables are tender. Add the saffron, Half & Half, and Maître d'Hôtel Butter. Whisk until smooth.

Put the potatoes into boiling water briefly (this is called parboiling), but don't overcook. Drain and set aside.

Gently poach the fish and/or seafood in the white wine, just until it's done (on poaching fish, see recipe for Seafood Cakes, p. 92).

When ready to serve, put some potatoes, fish, and so on in the bottom of each soup bowl, then pour in the hot soup. Sprinkle with cayenne pepper or paprika.

Pumpkin Soup

Tom wrote, "This is an unusual soup but one well worth trying."
8 servings

2 cups fresh pumpkin, diced, or
  1 ½ cups canned pumpkin
1 ½ quarts rich Chicken Stock
  (p. 24)
1 cup onions, chopped
3 cloves garlic
3 apples, peeled, cored,
  and cut into pieces
½ cup celery, chopped
2 tablespoons tomato paste

½ cup uncooked rice
½ teaspoon ground ginger
½ teaspoon cinnamon
¼ teaspoon ground clove
¼ teaspoon allspice
½ teaspoon white pepper
2 whole bay leaves
1 teaspoon A-1 Sauce
whipped cream, for garnish
nutmeg, for garnish

Cook the raw pumpkin in a covered double boiler until soft, then mash and press through a sieve. (Or use the canned stuff.) Bring the rest of the ingredients to a boil in a 3-quart pot, then simmer until the vegetables are soft and the rice is done, about 20 minutes. Remove the bay leaves, blend well in a blender, and return to the pot. Add the pumpkin, mix well, then taste for seasoning. Serve topped with a spoonful of unsweetened, whipped cream and a pinch of freshly grated nutmeg.

Puree of Bean
with Sherry Soup

8 servings

½ pound (I cup) red, white, and black beans

¼ pound salt pork, cut into tiny squares, or
⅛ pound bacon, chopped

2 onions, cut up

I carrot, cut up

I rib celery, cut up

I tablespoon tomato paste

2½ cups canned Italian tomatoes or 3–4 tomatoes, peeled (see Eggplant Provençal, p. 60), seeded, and chopped

2 whole cloves garlic

2 whole bay leaves

4 black peppercorns

2 cloves

¼ cup parsley, finely chopped

3 cups Chicken (p. 24) or Beef Stock (p. 22)

I cup (more or less) cooking sherry

salt, to taste

caramel coloring (see recipe for Beef Stock, p. 22) (optional)

sweet butter, for garnish

lemon or lime circles, for garnish

parsley, chopped, for garnish

good sherry, on the side

Soak the beans overnight and discard any that float to the top. Drain, saving 1 quart of the bean water.

Brown the salt pork or bacon in a 3-quart soup pot. Remove the meat and pour off most of the fat. Add the remaining ingredients, except the sherry, salt, and caramel coloring, including the beans and bean water. Cook until the beans are soft, about 3 hours. Remove the bay leaves and puree the mixture in a blender. Strain, then return to the pot. Add sherry to your taste. Thin with stock, if necessary, and taste for salt and seasoning. For a deep red color, add 1–2 drops of caramel coloring. Serve with teaspoon-sized dots of sweet butter and garnish with lemon or lime circles sprinkled with chopped parsley. Pass a cruet of good sherry.

Red Bean Soup

12 servings

1 pound (about 2 cups) red kidney beans

½ pound salt pork, cubed small

2 cups onions, finely chopped

1 cup celery, finely chopped

½ cup carrots, finely chopped

2 cloves garlic, finely chopped

1½ quarts Beef Stock (p. 22)

4 cloves

12 black peppercorns, cracked

2 whole bay leaves

2 tablespoons tomato paste

ham scraps, ham bone, ham hock, or a good chunk of stew beef with the bone

5 cups canned Italian tomatoes or 6–8 tomatoes, peeled (see Eggplant Provençal, p. 60), seeded, and chopped

1 cup cooking sherry

chopped green pepper, for garnish

chopped crisp bacon, for garnish

chopped parsley, for garnish

Wash the beans and soak overnight. Remove any beans that float. Drain, saving 1 quart of the bean water. Brown the salt pork in a soup kettle. Remove the pork and pour off most of the fat. Add the onions, celery, carrots, and garlic. Cook until brown, about 10 minutes. Add the stock, bean water, beans, cloves, peppercorns, bay leaves, tomato paste, and bone or meat. Cook until the beans are soft, about 4 hours. Add the tomatoes and sherry. Cook another 45 minutes to 1 hour. If the soup is too thin, blend and strain some of the beans, then return them to the pot. If it's too thick, thin it with some stock. Serve in soup plates with good sprinkles of a mixture of finely chopped green pepper, crisp bacon, and parsley.

Sausage Gumbo

The truth of the matter? This is actually Jerry Curtis's mother's recipe.

About 1 gallon

½ cup butter

6 tablespoons all-purpose flour

1 cup celery, chopped

½ cup onions, chopped

1 cup green peppers, chopped

½ pound smoked sausage, cubed

½ pound hot sausage, cubed, or, if available, Patton's Imitation Hot Sausage, pierced and boiled separately to remove the fat

1 or 2 whole bay leaves

½ teaspoon oregano

½ teaspoon leaf thyme

½ teaspoon basil

½ handful* chopped parsley

3 quarts Chicken Stock (p. 24)

1 tablespoon gumbo filé powder

salt and pepper, to taste

cooked rice, accompaniment

chopped parsley, for garnish

Melt the butter in a 5-quart pot over medium heat, then add the flour, stirring constantly, until it turns brown. Add everything else, except the stock and filé powder. Cook 5–10 minutes, then add the stock and filé powder. Simmer (do not boil) for an hour or so, skimming often. Serve in bowls with rice and sprinkles of chopped parsley.

*The secret to all good cooking is revealed—careful measurement!

Seafood Gumbo

12–16 servings

¾ cup butter
½ cup all-purpose flour
½ pound smoked sausage, cubed
¼ cup celery, chopped
½ cup onions, chopped
1 cup green peppers, chopped
1 whole bay leaf
½ teaspoon oregano
½ teaspoon leaf thyme
½ cup parsley, chopped
½ pound gumbo crabs or 1 fish bouillon cube

1 gallon shrimp stock (see Fish Stock, p. 25)
¾ teaspoon gumbo filé powder
salt and pepper, to taste
Kitchen Bouquet, for color (optional)
3–4 cups seafood (shrimp, mussels, oysters, etc.)
cooked rice, accompaniment
chopped parsley, for garnish

Melt the butter in a 6-quart pot over medium heat. Add the flour and cook, stirring constantly, until it turns brown. Add everything else, except the stock and filé powder. Cook until the onions are soft, then add the stock and filé powder. Simmer (do not boil—the filé powder will get stringy) for 30 minutes, taste for salt and pepper, then add Kitchen Bouquet. Add any seafood you wish, making sure not to overcook. Serve over cooked white rice with sprinkles of parsley.

Sorrel Soup

This soup is also delicious cold.

8–10 servings

½ pound salt pork, cubed
1½ cups onions, chopped
⅓ cup carrots, chopped
1 cup celery, chopped
2 whole cloves garlic
4 potatoes, peeled and chopped
1½ quarts rich Chicken Stock (p. 24)

1 pound fresh sorrel,* rinsed and deribbed
2 cups sorrel, rinsed, deribbed, and cut into strips
sour cream, for garnish
paprika, for garnish

Brown the salt pork in a 3-quart soup pot. Pour off most of the fat, leaving the salt pork. Add the remaining ingredients, except the sorrel strips. Cook over medium heat, stirring often, until the vegetables are soft, about 10 minutes. Remove the vegetables, blend well in the blender, then force through a sieve. Return to the pot. Thin with more stock, if necessary. Just before serving add the sorrel strips. Garnish with dollops of sour cream and dashes of paprika.

*For a variation, follow this recipe using spinach. The taste is quite different.

A good garnish for this is little pieces of hot, fried bacon.

Spicy Tomato Bouillon

8 servings

1 quart tomato juice

1 quart Chicken (p. 24) or Beef
  Stock (p. 22)

1 large onion, stuck with
6 cloves

16 black peppercorns

4 ribs celery, quartered

8 stems parsley

4 whole cloves garlic

3 whole bay leaves

1 cinnamon stick

½ teaspoon freshly scraped
  nutmeg

½ teaspoon allspice

½ teaspoon saffron

2 cups dry white wine or
  1 cup cooking sherry

peel of an orange or lemon

sour cream or whipped cream,
  for garnish

nutmeg, for garnish

Combine the ingredients in a 3-quart pot. Simmer for at least 2 hours.
Strain through cheesecloth or a fine sieve. Reheat, then serve in warm
consommé cups. Garnish each serving with a spoonful of sour cream
or unsweetened whipped cream and a grating of nutmeg.

Split Pea Soup

12 servings

1 pound (2 cups) split green peas	4 cloves
½ pound salt pork, cubed small	1 ½ quarts Chicken (p. 24) or Beef Stock (p. 22)
1 ½ cups onions, finely chopped	1 ham hock or ham bone
1 cup celery, finely chopped	2–3 dashes Tabasco
½ cup carrots, finely chopped	½ cup parsley, chopped
3 cloves garlic, finely chopped	1 ½ cups ham, chopped in small pieces
2 whole bay leaves	
6 black peppercorns	

Soak the peas overnight, remove any floaters, then drain. Brown the salt pork in a 3-quart soup pot over medium heat. Remove the pork and pour off most of the fat. Add the onions, celery, carrots, and garlic and cook until the vegetables are tender, about 10 minutes. Add the seasonings, stock, ham bone or hock, and peas. Cook until the peas are soft, about 2 hours. Remove the bay leaves and the ham bone or hock. Thin the soup with stock, if necessary. Add the Tabasco and most of the parsley. Reheat, then add the ham. Serve with sprinkles of parsley.

Vegetable Soup

Tom wrote, "This is the first soup I ever became aware of as it was one of my mother's favorites and one which, to my mind, she did to perfection. She would make it when the garden was in full harvest. We would have big bowls of it with hot yeast rolls and sweet, homemade butter from our cow Jerseyphine. Then, a big bowl of wilted lettuce, which my father would make. And for dessert an apple pie with good sharp cheddar or a fresh berry pie with heavy cream."

12 servings

2 tablespoons bacon, chicken, or beef fat

8 pieces short ribs or "heavy" beef

3 quarts water or half water and half Beef Stock (p. 22)

4 carrots, cut into large pieces

2 turnips, cut into large pieces

4 ribs celery, cut into large pieces

8 black peppercorns

3 whole cloves garlic

3 whole bay leaves

any vegetables you like, such as:
  green beans, cut up
  peas

carrots, cut in small pieces

potatoes, peeled and cut in small pieces

corn from the cob

fresh tomatoes, peeled (see Eggplant Provençal, p. 60), seeded, and chopped

small onions

okra, sliced

spinach or lettuce, cut fine

ground pepper and coarse salt, to taste

Heat the fat in a 5-quart soup pot over medium heat. Add the meat and sauté until browned. Add the water, stock, carrots, turnips, celery, peppercorns, garlic, and bay leaves and cook until the meat is tender, an hour or so, skimming and removing the fat as you go. Strain.

Remove the meat from the bones and cut into bite-size pieces. Return the meat and the strained soup to the pot. Now add whatever vegetables you have. Simmer until the vegetables are done but still slightly firm, about 15 minutes. Taste for salt and seasoning. Serve in large soup plates with freshly ground pepper and coarse salt.

Tom said, "Proust can have his cookie. I love my soup!"

Vichyssoise

4–6 servings

2 cups Cream Soup Base (p. 131)
1 cup heavy cream
1 cup Half & Half
pinch of nutmeg (optional)
salt, to taste
chives, freshly chopped or freeze-dried, for garnish

Combine the base, cream, and Half & Half. The soup should be the consistency of heavy cream. Add the nutmeg and salt to your taste. Serve very cold in chilled cups with generous sprinkles of chopped chives.

A lovely soup, hot or cold.

Sauces

Sauces

Béarnaise Sauce

Béarnaise Sauce

Tom wrote, "This sauce goes well with meats (see Tournedos Thomas, p. 253), but also try it with fried oysters. Or even scrod! You may be pleasantly surprised."

Béarnaise Base

About 2 cups

3 tablespoons shallots, minced
1/4 cup onions, minced
1 tablespoon dried tarragon
1/2 cup dry white wine
1/4 cup tarragon vinegar
1/2 teaspoon crushed black pepper
1 cup water

Put everything in a skillet and simmer, reducing it to a paste. Blend well, using a little more white wine if necessary, until the mixture forms a smooth paste. This base will keep for 2 weeks when refrigerated in a closed container.

Béarnaise Sauce

About 2½ cups

6 raw egg yolks
2 cups melted butter, cooled
1 tablespoon Béarnaise Base

1 tablespoon lemon juice

dash cayenne pepper (optional)

salt, to taste

Put the egg yolks in a glass or stainless steel bowl over hot (not boiling) water, and whisk until they triple in bulk. Slowly add the melted butter, beating constantly. Add the Béarnaise Base, lemon juice, and cayenne pepper. Taste for salt.

Blender Béarnaise

8 servings

8 raw egg yolks

2 tablespoons tarragon vinegar

1 small shallot

pinch tarragon leaves

¼ teaspoon white pepper

1 tablespoon water

4 cups hot clarified butter (see recipe for Barbecued Shrimp, p. 39)

Put everything but the butter in the blender. Blend briefly to mix the ingredients. While the blender is running, slowly add the butter. Keep adding the butter, turning the blender off and on, until the Béarnaise is the consistency of thick corn syrup. This will keep at 140° for up to 2 hours.

Carrot and Red Bell Pepper Salsa with Pecans

See Chicken Diablo (p. 208) or Panéed Garlic Fish (p. 234).

About 4 cups

1 medium red bell pepper, grated	2 tablespoons vegetable oil
4 medium carrots, grated	2 tablespoons lime juice
1 medium zucchini, grated	½ cup pecans, chopped
1½ tablespoons fresh ginger, grated	½ teaspoon black mustard seeds,* toasted
1 small red onion, grated	½ teaspoon sesame oil
1 jalapeño pepper, grated	
2 tablespoons rice wine vinegar	

Combine the ingredients in a large bowl. Chill.

*This item and many other wonderful ingredients are available at Asian markets.

Casino Sauce

This goes well with clams (see Clams Casino, p. 46), oysters, mussels, and so forth.

About 4 cups

> ¼ cup bacon grease or duck fat
> 1 ½ tablespoons garlic, minced
> 2 cups red bell peppers, minced
> 1 cup green bell peppers, minced
> ¾ cup red onions, minced
> 3 anchovy fillets, minced
> ½ tablespoon oregano
> 1 tablespoon fresh parsley, chopped

Heat the grease or fat in a skillet over medium heat. Add everything but the parsley into the pan. Cook just until the vegetables are tender, about 10 minutes. Add the parsley.

Cream Sauce

Cream Sauce

2 cups

2 tablespoons butter
2 tablespoons all-purpose flour
1 tablespoon sherry
1 ½ cups Half & Half
pinch white pepper
pinch powdered thyme
2 egg yolks
salt, to taste

Melt the butter in a double boiler, then stir in the flour. Add everything else but the egg yolks. Cook, but don't boil, stirring often, for 15 minutes. Add the egg yolks, then taste for salt. Continue stirring and cook for another 5 minutes.

Dijon Sauce

Dijon Sauce

See Rolatine of Chicken (p. 238).
2 cups

3 tablespoons butter
3 tablespoons all-purpose flour
1 cup Half & Half or heavy
   cream, preheated

2 chicken bouillon cubes,
   dissolved in
½ cup cooking sherry
pinch white pepper

pinch powdered thyme	(more or less, as desired)
½ teaspoon onion powder	2 raw egg yolks
2 tablespoons Dijon mustard	

Melt the butter in the top of a double boiler, add the flour and stir well for 2 minutes. Don't let it brown. Whisk in everything else except the egg yolks. Cook for 15 minutes or until the taste of flour is gone. Whisk in the yolks and cook, stirring, for another 5 minutes.

This sauce can be prepared a day ahead and reheated.

Cumberland Sauce

This is served with Chef's Country Pâté (p. 42) and also goes well with ham steaks.

4 cups

2 cups dry white wine	¾ cup currant jelly
½ cup balsamic vinegar	pinch tarragon
¾ cup orange juice	1 chicken bouillon cube
zest of 1 lemon	1 tablespoon dry mustard
zest of 1 orange	2 tablespoons cornstarch

Bring the wine, vinegar, and orange juice to a slow boil. Add the zest, jelly, tarragon, and bouillon cube. Dissolve the mustard and cornstarch in a little water and add to the sauce to thicken. Cook until corn-starch taste disappears.

Duck Sauces

Duck Stock

1 quart

duck trimmings, necks, gizzards, and livers
3 quarts water
6 chicken bouillon cubes
1 large onion, quartered
3 ribs celery, quartered
2 carrots, quartered
3 whole bay leaves

Put everything in a 5-quart stock pot and simmer for 2 hours or so, until the liquid has reduced to 1 quart. Strain, cool, then refrigerate. The fat will rise to the top and can easily be removed.

Keep the fat for sautéing vegetables and making sauces.

Port Sauce

About 4 cups

4 cups Duck Stock
2 tablespoons soy sauce
1/4 teaspoon black pepper
6 tablespoons port
3 tablespoons cornstarch
3-4 small whole cloves garlic
1/2 cup port

Heat the stock in a 2-quart pot over medium-high heat. Reduce by cooking to 3 cups, then add the soy sauce and black pepper. Combine the port and cornstarch and add to the stock. Cook until the sauce thickens. Strain and set aside. Put the garlic and additional port in a separate pot. Boil until the garlic is tender. Add to the sauce.

Fig Sauce

About 6 cups

duck drippings (see Roast Duck, p. 236)	2 teaspoons onion powder
	pinch of ginger
½ cup brandy	3 tablespoons currant jelly
24 dried figs	2 tablespoons orange juice
4 cups Duck Stock	concentrate
4 cups port	3 tablespoons lemon juice
½ teaspoon powdered thyme	3 tablespoons cornstarch
½ teaspoon white pepper	

Pour off the fat from the roasting pan, pour in the brandy, and scrape the pan clean (this is called deglazing). Put this goodness on the side. Slice the figs to make 48 circles and put in a large bowl. Put in the port and add the brandy deglazed material. Let soak overnight.

Drain the liquid from the soaked figs into a heavy, 2-quart saucepan. Add everything else, except the cornstarch. Stir over low heat until well blended. Put the figs into the sauce and cook slowly for 1 hour, or until the figs are soft. Mix the cornstarch with some cold water, making a paste. Stir this slowly and gently into the sauce until it is thick and clear and the cornstarch flavor is gone. (The entire amount of cornstarch may not be needed.) Remove from the fire, then reheat just before serving in a double boiler to avoid scorching. Covered carefully, it will keep well when refrigerated and, of course, can be frozen.

This Fig Sauce is also very good with baked ham.

Ginger Peach Sauce

About 5 cups

3 cups canned sliced peaches, drained
1 eight-ounce jar Major Grey Mango Chutney
2 teaspoons ginger, grated
3 tablespoons orange juice concentrate
2 tablespoons lemon juice
duck drippings (see Roast Duck, p. 236)
2 tablespoons cornstarch
2 teaspoons brandy
1 tablespoon currant jelly
2 fresh peaches, peeled and sliced

Put the canned peaches, chutney, ginger, concentrate, juice, and drippings in a heavy, 2-quart saucepan over medium heat. When hot, add the cornstarch mixed with the brandy. After the sauce thickens add the jelly and the peach slices. Cook for 5 more minutes.

Orange Sauce

About 5 cups

4 cups orange marmalade
½ 6-ounce can orange juice concentrate
1 tablespoon lemon juice
1 tablespoon currant jelly
¼ cup brandy
½ cup Grand Marnier
½–1 cup canned cranberries (optional)

Combine everything but the cranberries in a heavy, 2-quart saucepan over low heat just until it all mixes, about 10 minutes. Add cranberries, if you like.

Plum Sauce

About 5 cups

duck drippings (see Roast Duck, p. 236)

2 cups orange juice

2 six-ounce jars plum preserves

6 tablespoons red currant jelly

6 tablespoons ginger preserves

1 tablespoon lemon juice

1 teaspoon grated fresh ginger (optional)

3 tablespoons cornstarch

6 tablespoons plum brandy

1 cup fresh plums, pitted, or canned plums, drained

Pour the fat from the roasting pan. Add the orange juice, scrape the pan well, then reduce the liquid by cooking to ¾ cup, about 15 minutes. Put this into a heavy-bottomed, 2-quart saucepan. Add the preserves, jelly, lemon juice, and ginger. Bring to a boil, stirring (do not scorch!). Dissolve the cornstarch in the brandy. Add this to the boiling mixture, stirring constantly, until the mixture thickens and clears. If fresh plums are available, these can be pitted and added at this point. Canned plums may also be used.

This is very good served cold or hot with fresh pork, ham, sautéed chicken breast, or roasted chicken or turkey.

Garlic and Orange Salsa
Garlic and Orange Salsa

Serve this with Chicken Diablo (p. 208), Panéed Garlic Fish (p. 234), or shrimp. Experiment with the proportions.

2 cups

2–3 oranges, peeled, sectioned, seeded, and halved
¼ small jalapeño pepper, fresh or pickled, minced
1 teaspoon fresh cilantro, basil, or mint, chopped
½ teaspoon garlic, finely minced
1 tablespoon red onion, chopped
1 tablespoon rice wine vinegar
freshly ground black pepper, to taste
few drops sesame oil

Put everything but the sesame oil in a large bowl. Let stand for 1 hour, then strain, discarding the liquid. Stir in the sesame oil.

Honey Poached Garlic Sauce

This is delicious over vanilla ice cream (try it!) and over baked ham.

I cup garlic cloves, peeled
½ cup honey
½ cup water
pinch cinnamon
peel and juice of I orange
peel of I lemon

Combine the ingredients in a medium saucepan. Simmer gently until the water evaporates, about 25 minutes. Test for doneness after 20 minutes. The garlic should be tender, candied, and a light to medium nut-brown. If the garlic is done before the water evaporates, remove the cloves and cook the liquid until it is the consistency of honey. Chop or cut the cloves into thin slivers and recombine everything.

Hot Caper Sauce

Hot Caper Sauce

1 cup

¾ cup butter
1 onion, sliced
2 whole bay leaves
1 clove garlic, crushed
1 tablespoon Dijon mustard
1 anchovy fillet, mashed
1 ½ tablespoons lemon juice
3 tablespoons capers

Melt the butter in a double boiler. Add the onion, bay leaves, and garlic and cook for 30 minutes. Strain into a saucepan and put over fire until the butter bubbles and browns. Remove from the fire, then stir in the remaining ingredients. Reheat and pour generously over Salmon (or swordfish) Steaks (p. 244).

Lacombe Sauce

Lacombe Sauce

Serve over fettuccine or on sautéed trout or other fish.

1 serving

½ cup heavy cream
1 tablespoon green onions, chopped
2 tablespoons mushrooms, sliced

2 teaspoons dill weed

1 teaspoon salt

1 teaspoon black pepper

1 tablespoon brandy

5 shrimp, peeled and deveined, or 10 crawfish tails

Combine the ingredients in a saucepan over medium heat. If using shrimp, sauté them for 2 or 3 minutes first.

Madeira Sauce

This sauce goes well with escallops of veal with mushrooms. Or substitute lamb stock for the veal stock to serve with lamb.

About 5 cups

2 medium shallots, chopped

½ cup butter

1 teaspoon freshly cracked pepper

¼ cup all-purpose flour

1 quart hot veal stock (see Beef Stock, p. 22)

½ cup Madeira wine

salt and pepper, to taste

Kitchen Bouquet, for color

Sauté the shallots in the butter and pepper over medium heat in a heavy, 2-quart pot for 5 minutes. Slowly stir in the flour and cook, stirring constantly, until it turns brown. Add the stock and bring to a boil, then remove from the fire. Add the wine and taste for salt and pepper. Strain. Add Kitchen Bouquet for color.

Mango, Peach, and Apple Salsa

Serve with Chicken Diablo (p. 208) or Panéed Garlic Fish (p. 234).

About 8 cups

3 cups ripe peaches, chopped

¼ cup Pataka's Sweet Lime Pickle

1 ripe mango, peeled and chopped

1 Granny Smith apple, peeled and sliced into thin wedges

1 ripe pear, peeled and sliced into thin wedges

½ cup red bell pepper, chopped

12 radishes, thinly sliced and quartered

2 tablespoons fresh mint or basil, chopped

1 tablespoon fresh ginger, grated

2 tablespoons honey

Coarsely blend 1 cup of the peaches with the lime pickle. Combine all ingredients together in a bowl. Chill.

Marchand de Vin Sauce

See Tournedos Thomas (p. 253).

About 8 cups

½ cup shallots, minced
2 tablespoons garlic, minced
½ pound (about 3 cups) mushrooms, coarsely chopped
½ pound ham, coarsely chopped
1½ quarts Chicken Stock (p. 24)
2 whole bay leaves
1½ cups Burgundy
cornstarch, for thickening

Combine the ingredients, except for the wine and cornstarch, in a thick-bottomed, 3-quart saucepan. Cook over medium heat for 1 hour. Add the wine and cook for another 15 minutes. Thicken with a mixture of cornstarch dissolved in cold water. Keep warm.

Mole

See Chicken Empanada (p. 41).
About 6 cups

½ cup carrots, finely chopped
1 cup celery, finely chopped
1 ½ cups green peppers, finely chopped
1 ½ cups red peppers, finely chopped
3 jalapeño peppers, minced
1 ½ tablespoons garlic, chopped
1 apple, peeled and grated
½ cup pineapple juice
¼ cup orange juice concentrate
6 chicken bouillon cubes
1 cup water
2 ounces (2 squares) bitter chocolate
1 tablespoon (more or less, to taste) mole powder*

Combine everything but the chocolate and mole powder in a 3-quart saucepan over medium heat. Cook until the vegetables are soft, about 10 minutes. Add the chocolate and mole powder and stir until dissolved. Cool. Blend in a blender until smooth.

*If you can't find mole powder, combine in the following ratio: 1 part turmeric, 1 part black pepper, 1 part salt, 1 part cinnamon, 1/4–1/2 part cayenne pepper.

Mornay Sauce

Mornay Sauce

This sauce is delicious with fish (particularly trout, sole, or flounder), with just about any seafood, or in egg dishes. See Chicken Florentine (p. 210), Chicken Mornay (p. 214), Lobster Mornay (p. 229), Crabmeat Shostakovich (p. 55), and Swordfish with Mussels and Mushrooms (p. 250).

About 5 cups

½ cup sweet butter
3 tablespoons all-purpose flour
I cup rich Chicken (p. 24) or Fish Stock (p. 25)
I cup cream
I cup milk
¾ cup grated Parmesan cheese
pinch thyme
¼ teaspoon pepper
I cup (more or less, to your taste) cooking sherry
4 raw egg yolks
salt, to taste

Melt the butter in the top of a double boiler. Add the flour and stir well. Add the Chicken or Fish Stock, depending on the dish you have in mind. Stir, then add the other ingredients, except the egg yolks and salt. Stir well. Whisk in the egg yolks one at a time. Taste for salt.

Adding more stock to this sauce makes a wonderful, quick soup.

Pesto Sauce

Pesto Sauce, of course, works well on pasta or pizza, but it also goes well with meats, potatoes, and other vegetables. Experiment! It will keep well for weeks in a refrigerated, covered container.

About 4 cups

1 cup fresh basil, rinsed and dried, no stems
3–6 cloves garlic (to taste)
¾ cup pecans
½ cups grated Parmesan cheese
3 anchovy fillets
½ cup Italian parsley, no stems
1 cup good olive oil
1 tablespoon (more or less, to taste) balsamic vinegar, to taste
salt and pepper, to taste

Put everything but the oil, vinegar, and seasonings in a blender. Blend at a low speed (don't puree) for a moment. Slowly add the olive oil. Again, don't puree. Does it need perking? If so, add a little vinegar and taste for salt and pepper. Let it stand a few minutes, then taste it again.

Piquante Sauce

This works well with egg or seafood dishes.

About 5 cups

3 cups mayonnaise

1 raw egg yolk

¾ tablespoon dry mustard

¼ cup tomato paste (or more
   for color)

2 tablespoons parsley, chopped

2 tablespoons chives, chopped

2 tablespoons tarragon vinegar

½ cup sweet relish

¼ cup capers, chopped

2 dashes Tabasco

½ cup Pataka's Sweet Mustard
   Pickle, chopped

½ cup pimientos, blended

Combine the ingredients.

Ravigote Sauce

Serve with cold meats or fish.

About 4 cups

½ cup Bermuda onion, diced

1 cup parsley, stems removed,
   chopped

3 lemons, grated and juiced

3 cloves garlic, chopped

10 fresh basil leaves, chopped

1 teaspoon salt

2 tablespoons black pepper

1 teaspoon sugar

2 tablespoons Dijon mustard

¼ cup capers

½ cup tarragon vinegar

½ cup balsamic vinegar

2 cups olive oil

Combine the ingredients.

Red Bell Pepper Sauce

Red Bell Pepper Sauce

Use this sauce with Seafood Cakes (p. 92) or other seafood dishes.

About 6 cups

4 cups red bell peppers, seeded and finely chopped
1 cup red onion, finely chopped
1 clove garlic, crushed
½ cup dry white wine
1 tablespoon balsamic vinegar
1 tablespoon lemon juice
¼ jalapeño pepper, seeded and chopped

1 tablespoon cornstarch
1 two-inch piece fresh ginger, finely grated
½ cup cilantro, chopped
¼ cup good quality olive oil
pinch cayenne pepper
salt, to taste

Put the peppers, onions, garlic, wine, vinegar, juice, and jalapeño pepper in a 2-quart pot. Bring to a boil, then simmer until the vegetables are tender, about 20 minutes. Dissolve the cornstarch in a little cold water and add to the pot to bind the sauce. Cool. Puree. Add the ginger, cilantro mixed with olive oil, and cayenne. Taste for salt.

Rémoulade Sauce

This sauce works well with seafood (shrimp, soft-shell crabs, crawfish, lobster, etc.), chicken, avocados, and many vegetables. See Fried Artichoke Hearts (p. 63), Fried Green Tomatoes (p. 64), Scampi Rémoulade (p. 90), and Rolatine of Chicken (p. 238).

About 3 cups

1 pint mayonnaise (homemade, of course!)	4 sprigs parsley, leaves only, chopped
2 raw egg yolks	3 tablespoons lemon juice
2 tablespoons Dijon mustard	2 tablespoons good pickle relish
4 shallots, chopped	3 tablespoons sweet chili sauce
12 leaves fresh tarragon, chopped	4 dashes Tabasco
12 leaves fresh chervil, chopped	salt, to taste

Put half of the mayonnaise in a blender. Add the egg yolks, mustard, shallots, herbs, and lemon juice, then blend on high for 1 minute. Put the rest of the mayonnaise in a large bowl and add the blended ingredients, relish, chili sauce, and Tabasco. Mix well, tasting for salt and the sharpness desired.

Sauce Moutarde

Sauce Moutarde

This is the perfect dipping sauce for crab claws.

3½ cups

1½ cups mayonnaise
6 tablespoons sour cream
¼ cup dry white wine
2 tablespoons Dijon mustard
1 tablespoon Coleman's Dry
   Mustard
2 tablespoons yellow mustard

½ tablespoon sugar
1 teaspoon (more or less, to
   taste) lime or lemon juice
dash Tabasco
dash Worcestershire sauce
salt and white pepper, to taste

Combine the ingredients and chill.

Spicy Thai Sauce

This goes well with Soft-shell Crabs (p. 95) or Roast Duck (p. 236).

¾ cup

4 tablespoons red pepper jelly
1 tablespoon sesame oil
½ teaspoon chili oil
¼ cup rice wine vinegar
¼ teaspoon cinnamon
½ teaspoon garlic, chopped

6 fresh mint leaves, chopped
2 tablespoons fresh ginger, grated
2 tablespoons lime juice
1 teaspoon fish sauce (optional)

Combine the ingredients. Add the fish sauce last, or omit if serving with duck.

Thai Peanut Sauce

Thai Peanut Sauce

Serve at room temperature as a condiment with fish, chicken, or shrimp.

Variation 1

3 cups

18 ounces creamy peanut butter	3 tablespoons Worcestershire sauce
1 cup parsley, chopped	1 teaspoon cumin
1 tablespoon oregano	1 ½ teaspoons garlic, chopped
2 teaspoons hot chili oil	½ cup seasoned rice vinegar
2 tablespoons fresh ginger, chopped	1 tablespoon soy sauce

Combine the ingredients.

Variation 2

1 ½ cups

9 ounces creamy peanut butter	1 tablespoon honey
1 teaspoon hot chili oil	½ teaspoon fish sauce
1 teaspoon fresh ginger, grated	½ teaspoon salt
1 teaspoon garlic, minced	¾ teaspoon simbal*
2 tablespoons rice vinegar	1 teaspoon brown sugar
1 teaspoon soy sauce	6 tablespoons lime juice

Combine the ingredients.

*Simbal is *very hot* pepper relish that is available at Chinese markets. Use sparingly and be careful about getting it on your skin (it's that hot!).

Tomatillo Salsa

Serve with Chicken Diablo (p. 208) or Panéed Garlic Fish (p. 234).
About 1 1/2 cups

12 tomatillos (golf ball-size)
4–6 tablespoons rice wine vinegar
1 chicken bouillon cube
1/2–1 cup (or more, to taste) cilantro, chopped
salt and pepper, to taste

Wash the tomatillos and cut them each in half. Put them into a food processor. Puree, adding a little water, if necessary, to make it smooth. Put into a 3-cup saucepan. Add the vinegar and bouillon cube. Put over a medium fire and reduce by cooking until it bubbles and thickens (so it's not watery). Chill over ice. When cold, add the cilantro. Taste for salt and pepper.

Tartar Sauce

Tartar Sauce

Variation 1

1½ cups

1 cup mayonnaise
¼ cup sweet pickle relish
2 tablespoons onions, finely minced
4 teaspoons green peppers, finely minced
4 teaspoons parsley, chopped
1 teaspoon onion powder
1 dash Tabasco
4 teaspoons lemon juice

Combine the ingredients.

Variation 2

About 2 cups

1½ cups mayonnaise
½ cup dill pickle relish
2 hard-boiled egg yolks, pushed through a sieve
3 pieces crisp bacon, crumbled
¼ cup onions, finely chopped
2 dashes Tabasco
3 tablespoons lemon juice
pinch of salt

Combine the ingredients.

White Rémoulade Sauce

White Rémoulade Sauce

This goes well with cold egg or shrimp dishes.

About 6 cups

1 quart mayonnaise	¼ cup capers, chopped
1 tablespoon onion powder	½ tablespoon caper liquid
½ tablespoon white pepper	2 hard-boiled eggs,
¼ tablespoon dry mustard	finely chopped
2 tablespoons lemon juice	2 tablespoons dried parsley
concentrate	¼ tablespoon black pepper
¾ teaspoon Tabasco	½ cup milk
4 teaspoons fresh tarragon	¼ cup heavy cream
leaves, chopped	

Combine the ingredients. Add a little more milk, if necessary, for a smooth but not runny consistency.

In the middle of a chaotic Saturday night rush at Upperline Restaurant, when everyone in the kitchen was exhausted, Tom would sneak upstairs and put on this mask, then stand at the top of the stairs, aproned stomach thrust out, hands on hips, posing. Within seconds the whole staff would be laughing.

Entrees

Baked Stuffed Striped Sea Bass

8–10 servings

1 five- to six-pound sea bass
kosher salt
coarse cracked black pepper
½ clove garlic, crushed
½ teaspoon leaf thyme
½ cup sweet butter
1 cup onions, finely chopped
1 cup celery, finely chopped
½ cup white seedless raisins,
    soaked in white wine
2½ cups bread, toasted and
    cubed
½ teaspoon powdered thyme
1 cup parsley, chopped
salt and pepper, to taste

¼ cup sweet butter, melted
2 whole bay leaves
3 slices onion
1 cup white wine
¼ cup sweet butter, softened
3 tablespoons lemon juice
all-purpose flour,
    for thickening
melted butter, for thickening
½ cup parsley, chopped
egg white, for a glaze
boiled new potatoes,
    accompaniment
lemon wedges, for garnish
parsley sprigs, for garnish

Clean the fish. Leave whole (remove the head, if you wish). Wash it thoroughly and pat dry. Rub the inside of the fish with a mixture of kosher salt, pepper, garlic, and leaf thyme. Melt ½ cup butter in a large skillet over medium heat, then add the onions and celery and cook for 5–6 minutes, or until the vegetables are transparent. Add the raisins, bread, powdered thyme, and parsley. Toss gently and taste for salt and pepper. Loosely stuff the fish with this mixture.

Make a boat from heavy-duty aluminum foil to hold the fish. Put the ¼ cup melted butter, bay leaves, onion, and wine in the bottom of the boat. Place the fish on top and dot with ¼ cup softened sweet butter. Close and seal the foil, making sure the ends of the boat are secure so the liquid won't escape. Put on a rack in a baking pan.

Bake in a 375° oven for 1 hour, basting frequently, testing for doneness after 45 minutes. The fish is done when it is opaque all the way through (check by parting the flesh slightly). Don't overcook! When done, remove from the oven, pour the liquid into a small saucepan, and add the lemon juice. Thicken with mixture of flour and melted butter. Add the parsley, stir well, and keep the sauce hot.

Brush the fish with egg white and, with the foil open, put in a hot 500° oven for 10 minutes. This will make a nice glaze. Carefully remove and place the fish on a hot platter. Pour over the sauce and garnish with wedges of lemon, boiled new potatoes, and bunches of parsley sprigs.

Bagna Cauda

About 2½ cups

¼ cup butter	½ teaspoon Dijon mustard
¼ cup olive oil	2 tablespoons mashed Roasted
15 cloves garlic, finely chopped	Garlic (p. 88)
4 ounces (20–25) anchovy	cooked ziti or penne pasta,
fillets, chopped	accompaniment
1 quart heavy cream	carrots, in matchstick slices,
1 teaspoon garlic, chopped	for garnish

Heat the butter and oil in a 2-quart saucepan. Add the garlic and cook until it starts to take on color. Add the anchovies and cook until they're dissolved. (You may stop here and use this mixture as a vegetable dip or serve it with boiled beef or chicken.) Add the cream and reduce by half, stirring often. Add the remaining ingredients and keep hot. Serve over ziti or penne pasta, topped with generous sprinkles of just-cooked, sliced carrots.

Bayou Barbecued Shrimp and Oysters with Fettuccine

4 servings

½ cup butter	salt and pepper, to taste
¼ pound shrimp shells	16–24 shrimp, peeled and
2 whole cloves garlic	deveined
2 tablespoons all-purpose flour	16–24 oysters, shucked
1 quart hot oyster broth	butter, for sautéing
1 whole bay leaf	cooked fettuccine,
1 fish bouillon cube	accompaniment
3–4 tablespoons Crystal	fresh basil, julienne strips,
Louisiana Hot Sauce	for garnish

Melt the butter in a 2-quart pot over medium heat. Add the shells and garlic and sauté until golden brown. Add the flour, stir well, and cook for 1 minute (do not burn). Add the broth, bay leaf, bouillon cube, and hot sauce. Bring to a boil, whisking, then simmer for 20 minutes. Taste for salt and pepper, then strain and keep hot.

When ready to serve, sauté the shrimp and oysters in a large skillet in a little butter for 1 minute. Pour in the hot sauce and cook for another 3–4 minutes. Don't overcook! Serve over fettuccine and sprinkle with strips of fresh basil.

Blowfish in White Wine Sauce

6 servings

1 cup all-purpose flour	3 tablespoons butter
1 tablespoon dry mustard	2 tablespoons all-purpose flour
½ teaspoon mace	1 cup Fish Stock (p. 25)
1 teaspoon paprika	3 egg yolks
1 tablespoon salt	pinch powdered thyme
½ teaspoon white pepper	3 tablespoons lemon juice
6 blowfish fillets,* or use	1 cup heavy cream, whipped
flounder, sole, or other	salt and pepper, to taste
fine-textured fish	parsley sprigs, for garnish
milk	lemon wedges, for garnish
butter, for sautéing	

Combine the flour with the other dry ingredients. Dip the fish fillets in milk, then roll in the flour mixture. Sauté in a little butter, then place on a warm serving platter. Melt the butter in a double boiler, add everything but the lemon juice and cream, and cook until smooth and thickened. Now add the juice and cream and taste for salt and pepper. Pour the sauce over the fish, sprinkle with chopped parsley, and garnish with lemon wedges and sprigs of parsley.

*Be sure the liver and ovaries are removed as they are poisonous!

Broiled Shad Roe

3–4 servings

½ cup butter	2 dashes Tabasco
1 tablespoon bacon fat	3 tablespoons lemon juice
1 anchovy fillet, mashed	1 shad roe
½ clove garlic, crushed	Seasoned Flour (p. 27)
1 small onion, grated	Maître d'Hôtel Butter,
½ teaspoon fresh tarragon,	for garnish (p. 26)
chopped	lemon, for garnish
1 teaspoon parsley, chopped	
1 teaspoon fresh chervil,	
chopped	

Melt the butter and bacon fat in a saucepan. Add the anchovy, garlic, onion, and herbs, and cook slowly until the onions are transparent, not browned, about 5 minutes. Remove from the fire and add the Tabasco and lemon juice.

Wipe the roe carefully with a damp cloth and prick several times with a needle (to prevent bursting). Brush with the herb butter and roll in Seasoned Flour.

Place on an oiled broiler plate and put under the broiler for a total of 10–15 minutes (depending on its size), carefully turning it once, brushing occasionally with the herb butter. (You may prefer to sauté the roe. If so, cook over low heat for 10–15 minutes, carefully turning once. Don't cook it too fast or it will burst.) When done remove to a hot plate. Garnish with Maître d'Hôtel Butter and wedges of lemon.

Broiled Striped Sea Bass

1 serving

> 1 striped sea bass fillet or other firm-textured fish
> a generous swipe Maître d'Hôtel Butter (p. 26)
> 2 or 3 thin slices onion
> 1 whole bay leaf
> paprika, for color
> ¼–½ cup dry white wine
> chopped parsley, for garnish
> lemon wedge, for garnish
> parsley sprigs, for garnish

Filet (or have your fishmarket person filet) the bass and cut it into desired portions, about ⅓–½ pound per person. On a flat pan that will fit under the broiler put the Maître d'Hôtel Butter, onions, and bay leaf. Place the fish on top of this, brush generously with more Maître d'Hôtel Butter, then sprinkle lightly with paprika. Since the sea bass tends to be dry, pour some white wine around the fish.

Place the fish under the broiler 3 inches from the flames and broil for 5 minutes. Spoon the hot butter mixture over the fish and return to the flame for another 5 minutes. If the fillet is thick, it may take another minute or so. Test the fish by parting the flesh slightly with a fork to see if it has lost its transparency.

When done, remove it to a hot plate and spoon on some of the luscious liquid. Sprinkle lightly with chopped parsley and garnish with a large wedge of lemon and a sprig of parsley.

Calf's Liver à l'Orange

14 ounces good quality orange
  marmalade
1 tablespoon orange juice
  concentrate
2 tablespoons brandy
2 tablespoons Grand Marnier
1 teaspoon red currant jelly
1 teaspoon lemon juice
1/8 teaspoon powdered thyme
  (optional)
1–1 1/2 pounds liver, sliced
  1/4 to 1/3 inch thick

Seasoned Flour (p. 27) or
  corn flour
oil or clarified butter (see
  Barbecued Shrimp, p. 39), for
  sautéing
4 orange slices, dipped in sugar
8 slices crisp cooked bacon
  (optional)
Dijon mustard
watercress, for garnish

Combine the first seven ingredients in a 3-cup saucepan. Bring to a boil, then simmer for 2 minutes. Dust the liver with the flour, then sauté in oil or clarified butter in a hot skillet. When done, remove to warm plates. Dip the orange slices in sugar and cook quickly in the same pan as the liver, adding a little more butter, if necessary. Place on top of the liver, pour over 1–2 tablespoons of the sauce, and top with the bacon slices. Serve with a dab of Dijon mustard and a sprig of watercress, with extra sauce on the side.

"This is sheer brilliance. It will make liver lovers freak out and may easily convert the armies of liver haters. The dish best demonstrates Chef Cowman's very special talent for merging meat, fowl, or fish with fruit."—Richard Collin, "Jonathan: A New Orleans Treasure," *Figaro*, May 17, 1978, sect. 2, p. 9.

Chicken with Almonds

6 servings

3 whole broiling chickens, about 2½ pounds each	3 tablespoons lemon juice
	1 teaspoon yellow mustard
2 cups Chicken Stock (p. 24)	½ teaspoon ginger
1 cup dry white wine	½ pound almonds
salt and pepper, to taste	butter, for sautéing
butter	parsley sprigs, for garnish
paprika, for color	lemon wedges, for garnish
¾ cup honey	

Wash the chickens well in cold water, then pat dry. Cut in half, remove the wing tips, and trim off the leg ends. Arrange in a shallow roasting pan, breast side up. Pour in the stock and white wine, sprinkle with salt and pepper, dot with butter, and dust with paprika.

Bake at 425° for 40 minutes, basting often after the first 20 minutes. When done, remove from the oven and, using a baster, transfer the liquid in the pan to a 2-cup saucepan. Reduce by cooking over a high heat to about ½ cup. Allow the birds to cool a bit, then gently pull out the back and rib bones, making the chicken a bit easier to eat.

Combine the honey, juice, mustard, and ginger in a bowl. Add to the reduced roasting pan liquid. Brush the birds with this and return them to the oven to cook for 20 more minutes, brushing with the honey mixture twice more, or until the mixture is all used. The chickens should have a nice, golden glaze at the end of the cooking time.

While the chicken is cooking pour boiling water over the almonds to remove the skins. (This is called blanching.) Sliver the almonds, then sauté in butter until golden brown. Keep warm.

When the chickens are done, remove them to a heated platter or individual plates and dress with the almonds, wedges of lemon, and sprigs of parsley.

Brussels sprouts are a good accompaniment to this.

Chicken Burgundy

6 servings

3 whole frying chickens, cut up	1 tablespoon currant jelly
butter, for sautéing	1 cup Chicken Stock (p. 24)
1 cup brandy	6 cups (more or less) Burgundy
18 whole small white onions	1 whole bay leaf
18 mushroom caps	all-purpose flour, for thickening
1 small onion, finely chopped	melted butter, for thickening
1 carrot, finely chopped	chopped parsley, for garnish
1 clove garlic, crushed	chopped chives, for garnish
1 tablespoon tomato paste	

Brown the chicken pieces in butter in a large, heavy skillet. Pour in the brandy, then transfer everything to a casserole. Brown the onions in the same skillet. Add to the casserole.

Sauté the mushrooms in a little butter in a clean skillet and add them to the casserole. Brown the chopped onion, carrot, and garlic in the same skillet. Stir in the tomato paste, jelly, and stock, heat briefly, then pour over the chicken. Cover the chicken with Burgundy and add the bay leaf. Cover and put in a 350° oven for 1 hour or until tender. Thicken the liquid with flour mixed equally with butter. Serve with sprinkles of chopped parsley and chopped chives.

Chicken Cacciatore

6 servings

3 whole frying chickens, cut up
butter, for sautéing
½ cup salt pork, diced
2 onions, roughly chopped
1 carrot, roughly chopped
1 rib celery, roughly chopped
2 cloves garlic
1 cup red wine (Chianti)
1 twenty-eight-ounce can Italian
  plum tomatoes or 4 cups

tomatoes, peeled (see
  Eggplant Provençal, p. 60),
  seeded, and chopped
flour, for thickening
melted butter, for thickening
¼ cup fresh basil, chopped
¼ cup parsley, chopped
grated Parmesan cheese,
  on the side

Brown the chicken pieces in butter in a large, heavy skillet. Put into a casserole. Brown the salt pork, onions, carrot, celery, and garlic in another skillet, then pour over the chicken. Add the wine, cook for 30 minutes over a low flame, then add the tomatoes and cook until the chicken is tender, about 20 more minutes. Thicken the sauce with a blend of butter and flour, then add most of the basil and parsley. Sprinkle chopped basil on top and grated cheese on the side. Serve with rice and green peas or Italian beans.

Chicken with Cherries

Chicken with Cherries

6 servings

3 whole frying chickens, cut up	l whole bay leaf
butter, for sautéing	l tablespoon currant jelly
½ cup onions, chopped, or	l teaspoon lemon juice
2 tablespoons shallots,	l cup port
chopped	cornstarch, mixed with water,
l clove garlic, chopped	for thickening
l cup port	l ½ cups pitted cherries
½ cup brandy	parsley sprigs, for garnish
l cup Chicken Stock (p. 24)	watercress sprigs, for garnish

Brown the chicken in butter in a large, heavy skillet, then remove to a casserole. Sauté the onions or shallots and garlic for a few minutes in the same skillet. Add the port, brandy, and stock. Pour over the chicken and add the bay leaf.

Put in a 350° oven for 50 minutes or until the chicken is tender, then remove the chicken to a platter. Strain the liquid (should be about 1 cup) into a 1-quart saucepan, add the jelly, lemon juice, and port, and cook for a few minutes, thickening with cornstarch mixed with water. Cook until the sauce clears, add the cherries, and heat through. Pour over the chicken and garnish with sprigs of parsley or watercress.

Chicken Curry Bombay

8 servings

3–4 chicken breasts or
   1 whole chicken, cut up
½ cup (more or less) Seasoned
   Flour (p. 27)
butter, for sautéing
curry powder
1 cup onions, finely chopped
1 cup celery, finely chopped
1 cup green apples, peeled,
   seeded, and chopped
½ cup white seedless raisins
2 cloves garlic, crushed
2 tablespoons curry powder
   (or more, to your taste)

1 teaspoon ginger
½ teaspoon allspice
1 cup apple cider
2 cups Chicken Stock (p. 24)
2 whole bay leaves
2 cups sour cream
salt, to taste
cornstarch, mixed with stock,
   for thickening
cooked saffron rice,
   accompaniment
curry condiments,
   accompaniment

Dust the chicken with Seasoned Flour and a little curry powder and brown in a skillet in butter. Take it out of the skillet and remove the meat from the bones, putting the meat to the side. Add the onions, celery, apples, raisins, and garlic to the skillet and cook for 10 minutes, stirring often. Add the spices, cider, stock, bay leaves, and chicken, and simmer for 1 hour. Remove the bay leaves, stir in the sour cream, and taste for curry and salt. The sauce should be thick enough to coat a spoon. If not, thicken with cornstarch dissolved in stock. Serve with fluffy saffron rice and pass a tray with any or all of the following condiments: chopped, crisp bacon; orange zest; sliced bananas; chopped peanuts; shredded coconut; sliced pineapple; lemon zest; raisins; currants; mango chutney; sliced cherry tomatoes.

Chicken Diablo

Tom was awarded a special plaque by the American Heart Association for contributing this heart-healthy recipe.

1 serving

1 boneless chicken breast, skin removed
1 tablespoon Dijon mustard
1 teaspoon sesame oil
½ teaspoon fresh ginger, grated
5–8 dashes Tabasco
2 tablespoons lime juice

Trim and clean the chicken, then marinate it for 1 hour in a mixture of the remaining ingredients. Grill over hot charcoal, preferably, or broil until done, about 5–6 minutes on each side. Serve with any or a variety of the following salsas: Carrot and Red Bell Pepper with Pecans (p. 168); Garlic and Orange (p. 176); Mango, Peach and Apple (p. 180); or Tomatillo (p. 191).

Chicken Dijon

6 servings

3 whole frying chickens, cut up	1 cup dry white wine
butter, for sautéing	2 whole bay leaves
1 cup onions, finely chopped	2 cups sour cream
½ cup celery, finely chopped	salt and pepper, to taste
2 cloves garlic, mashed	cornstarch, for thickening
4 tablespoons Dijon mustard	stock, for thickening
1 cup Chicken Stock (p. 24)	

Brown the chicken in butter in a large, heavy skillet and remove to a casserole. Sauté the onions, celery, and garlic in the same skillet until they turn transparent, about 5 minutes. Add the mustard, stock, and wine. Pour this over the chicken and add the bay leaves. Cover and cook on the stove for 45 minutes or until tender. Remove the chicken to a platter and keep warm.

Strain the liquid into a 1-quart saucepan and reduce by cooking over high heat to 1 cup. Add the sour cream and more Dijon mustard, if desired. Taste for salt and pepper and thicken with some cornstarch mixed with stock, if necessary. Pour the sauce over the chicken, reserving some for passing in a sauce boat.

New potatoes tossed in butter and chopped fresh dill go well with this.

Chicken Florentine

Chicken Florentine

4 servings

2 cups cooked fresh or frozen spinach, well drained
4 cups Mornay Sauce (p. 183)
4 cups boiled chicken (see Chicken Stock, p. 24)
1 cup grated Parmesan cheese
paprika, for color
broiled tomatoes
bread crumbs, for garnish
Parmesan cheese, for garnish

Put a layer of spinach in the bottoms of individual casseroles. Cover with a layer of Mornay Sauce, then a layer of chicken, then more Mornay Sauce. Sprinkle with the grated Parmesan cheese and dust with paprika. Heat in a 425° oven until the sauce bubbles and browns. Serve with a broiled half tomato that's been sprinkled with bread crumbs mixed with grated Parmesan cheese.

Chicken with Ham and Cheddar

4 servings

4 cups Mornay Sauce (p. 183)
1 pound cooked ham, thinly sliced
2 pounds boiled chicken, sliced (see Chicken Stock, p. 24)
12 thin slices tomato
1 cup good sharp cheddar cheese, grated
cooked spinach (optional)

Layer in the following order into individual casseroles: sauce, ham, sauce, chicken, sauce. Top each casserole with 3 tomato slices and sprinkle with grated cheese. Bake at 425° until the sauce bubbles and browns. Spinach is good with this and may be added as another layer.

Chicken with Ham and Pâté

6 servings

½ cup dry white wine	butter, for sautéing
½ cup cooking sherry	1 cup cooking sherry
2 whole bay leaves	all-purpose flour, for thickening
1 onion, sliced	butter, melted, for thickening
2 cups Chicken Stock (more or less) (p. 24)	6 garlic croutons*
3 tablespoons lemon juice	6 thin slices pâté
6 squab chickens or half a broiling chicken per person	6 thin slices cooked ham
36 small whole mushrooms	green peas, for garnish
	small (pearl) onions, for garnish
	watercress sprigs, for garnish

Put the wine, sherry, bay leaves, onion slices, 1 cup of the stock, and lemon juice in a roasting pan, then put in the chickens. Bake at 425°, basting a few times, for 45 minutes or until the chickens are tender. Remove the chickens to a warm platter, saving the juices. If broiling chickens are being used, remove the ribs and back bones carefully, so they remain intact.

To make the mushroom sauce, sauté the mushrooms in a little butter in a 2-quart saucepan. Remove the mushrooms and pour in the roasting pan juices. Add enough stock to make about 3 cups of liquid. Add the sherry and cook over medium heat for 5 minutes. Thicken with melted butter and flour mixed in equal parts. Add the mushrooms.

On garlic croutons spread a thin layer of pâté. Add a layer of ham, then spoon on some of the sauce. Put the bird on next and pour on more mushroom sauce. Garnish with peas, small onions, and sprigs of watercress.

*Garlic croutons are slices of crustless bread fried to a golden brown in olive oil in which garlic has been cooked.

Crawfish Jonathan

12 servings

2 medium-sized eggplants, diced and salted
1 cup olive oil
1 cup onions, diced small
2 cloves garlic, finely chopped
2 cups green peppers, diced small
1½ cups celery, diced small
1 jalapeño pepper, finely chopped
1 cup carrots, finely chopped
3 chicken bouillon cubes
½ cup cooking sherry
1 teaspoon tomato paste
1 cup V-8 Juice

3 cups tomatoes, peeled (see Eggplant Provençal, p. 60), seeded, and chopped
1 teaspoon leaf thyme
dash Tabasco
dash Worcestershire sauce
1 pound cooked crawfish tails, with any available fat
1 cup bread crumbs
grated Parmesan cheese
chopped parsley
paprika, for color
cooked whole crawfish, for garnish
lemon wedges, for garnish

Dice the eggplants into small pieces and sprinkle with salt. Let stand for 30 minutes, then rinse and squeeze dry.

Heat the oil in a large skillet, add the vegetables, and cook for 5 minutes, stirring often. Add the bouillon cubes dissolved in the sherry, tomato paste, tomatoes, V-8, thyme, Tabasco, and Worcestershire. Cook over low heat for a while. Stir in the eggplant and heat until cooked, but not soft, about 5–6 minutes. Add V-8 Juice if the mixture is too dry. Add the crawfish tails and cook for 10 minutes, or until well heated. Remove from the fire. Add most of the bread crumbs.

Put into individual ramekins (or one large casserole). Sprinkle with the rest of the bread crumbs, grated Parmesan cheese, chopped parsley, and a little paprika for color. Reheat when ready to serve and garnish with cooked whole crawfish and wedges of lemon.

Chicken Mornay with Asparagus or Broccoli

8 servings

1 four- to five-pound boiling
  chicken or capon

2 whole cloves garlic

1 large onion, quartered

2 ribs celery, quartered

2 carrots, quartered

1 small bunch parsley

10 black peppercorns

2 whole bay leaves

2 quarts (or more) Chicken
  Stock (p. 24)

½ cup sweet butter

3 tablespoons all-purpose flour

3 egg yolks, separate

1 cup cooking sherry

1 cup heavy cream, whipped

salt and pepper, to taste

32–48 asparagus spears or
  broccoli pieces, cooked in
  stock

1¾ cups grated Parmesan
  cheese

paprika, for color

Wash and cut up the chicken and put into a 6-quart pot. Add the garlic, vegetables, parsley, peppercorns, and bay leaves. Cover with stock. Cook slowly, skimming occasionally and removing the fat. When the chicken is done (but not falling off the bones, about 45 minutes), remove it from the pot, let it cool, then slice. Strain the stock and reduce by cooking to make 1 quart. Melt the butter in a double boiler, then stir in the flour. Slowly add 3 cups of the stock, the egg yolks one at a time (whisking constantly), then the sherry and cream. The sauce should be nicely thickened. Taste for salt and pepper.

Pour a little of the sauce into 8 individual casseroles, enough to cover the bottoms. Place 4–6 cooked asparagus spears or broccoli pieces in each dish, with the tips pointed toward the ends of the dishes. Put in some more sauce, then a layer of the sliced chicken. Add most of the Parmesan cheese (saving some for the top) to the remainder of the sauce and mix well. Cover the chicken with this, letting the vegetable tips show. Dust with the rest of the grated cheese and a little paprika. Bake at 450° until the sauce bubbles and browns. Serve with saffron rice and French Style Green Peas.

French Style Green Peas

8 servings

4 cups fresh green peas, shelled
1 tablespoon butter
1 cup Chicken Stock (p. 24)
a little grated onion, to taste
lettuce leaves

Put the peas, butter, stock, and onion in a skillet. Cover with lettuce and steam until tender. Remove the lettuce and serve.

Chicken Normandy

6 servings

3 two-and-one-half-pound broiling chickens	1½ cups applesauce
all-purpose flour	3 tablespoons lemon juice
salt	salt and pepper, to taste
pepper	1 cup sour cream
paprika	½ cup grated Romano or Parmesan cheese
½ cup butter	all-purpose flour, for thickening
½ cup applejack or calvados	melted butter, for thickening
1½ cups Chicken Stock (p. 24)	butter, for sautéing
¼ cup sweet butter	apple rings, for garnish
1 cup onions, finely chopped	nutmeg
½ cup celery, finely chopped	sugar
½ clove garlic, mashed	cinnamon

Wash and dry the chickens, trim away the wing and leg tips, then cut in quarters. Dust with flour, salt, pepper, and paprika. Melt the butter in a large, heavy-bottomed skillet. Heat until it just begins to bubble. Fry the chicken pieces until they have a nice color. Remove to a baking pan. Pour the applejack or calvados into the skillet, then ignite the liquid carefully with a long match and allow it to burn out. Add ½ cup of the chicken stock. Scrape the pan well, then strain this goodness into a bowl. In the same skillet melt the sweet butter. Add the onion, celery, and garlic. Cook until transparent and golden, but not brown. Stir in the applesauce and lemon juice, then add 1 cup of stock and the reserved pan juices. Taste for salt and pepper. Cook for a few minutes, then pour the mixture over the chicken, coating it well.

Place in a 400° oven and bake for 40 minutes or until the chicken is tender. Remove the chicken to a hot platter to keep warm. Add the sour cream and grated cheese to the baking pan. Mix well. If the sauce is too thin, thicken it with a little butter mixed equally with flour. Pour the sauce over the chicken. Garnish with apple rings fried in butter and sprinkled with nutmeg, sugar, and a little cinnamon.

Court Bouillon

About 12 servings

½ cup butter	1½ cups dry white wine
2 cups onions, chopped	3–5 pounds firm white-fleshed
1½ cups celery, chopped	fish (bass, drum, etc.)
3 whole cloves garlic	2½ cups tomatoes, chopped
1 cup carrots, chopped	1 small bunch parsley, stems
12 black peppercorns, crushed	removed
3 whole bay leaves	chopped parsley, for garnish
2 quarts water or Fish Stock	steamed rice, accompaniment
(p. 25)	(optional)

Melt the butter over medium heat in a 5-quart pot. Add the onions, celery, garlic, carrots, peppercorns, and bay leaves. Cook for 10–15 minutes or until the vegetables are browned. Add the water (or stock) and wine and scrape the pan well. Simmer for 5 minutes.* Add the fish and tomatoes and poach (see Seafood Cakes, p. 92) until the fish is done. Add the parsley. Serve by itself or with some steamed white rice in a bowl or deep dish and garnish with chopped parsley.

*At this point you may continue to cook this for about an hour, then strain it through a fine sieve and use it as a rich Fish Stock for poaching fish (see Poached Salmon, p. 235, and Swordfish with Mussels and Mushrooms, p. 250.)

Crab Supreme

8 servings

1 cup sweet butter	1 cup heavy cream
2 tablespoons shallots, chopped,	½ cup sherry
or ½ cup onions, chopped	3 egg yolks
4 cups mushrooms, very thinly	½ cup grated Parmesan cheese
sliced	3 tablespoons lemon juice
2 cups dry white wine	salt and pepper, to taste
½ cup good sherry	buttered toast, accompaniment
2 cups fresh crabmeat, picked	chopped parsley, for garnish
clean of shells	peas with pimiento,
3 tablespoons all-purpose flour	accompaniment (optional)

Melt ½ cup butter in a skillet. Add the shallots or onions and gently sauté. When transparent, add the mushrooms, wine, and sherry. Cover and cook for 10 minutes. Add the crabmeat. Cook 5 more minutes. Remove from the heat and strain, keeping the liquid and the mushrooms.

Melt another ½ cup butter in a double boiler. Add the flour and stir until smooth. Add the mushroom/crab liquid (should be about 1 cup), cream, sherry, and egg yolks. Whisk well until thick and smooth. Add the Parmesan cheese and lemon juice, taste for salt and pepper, then add the crabmeat and mushrooms. Cook 5 minutes more. Serve immediately on hot buttered toast with sprinkles of chopped parsley.

Peas with pimiento added is a good accompaniment.

Creamed Scallops with Mushrooms and Bacon

8 servings

1½ cups dry white wine	good dash good sherry
2 cups mushrooms, thinly sliced	salt and pepper, to taste
1 quart bay scallops	buttered toast or cooked rice,
½ cup sweet butter	accompaniment
2 shallots, finely chopped	1 cup (or more) bacon,
2 tablespoons all-purpose flour	chopped, for garnish
1 cup heavy cream	½ cup chives, chopped, for garnish
4 egg yolks, separate	paprika, for color

Heat the wine over medium heat in a 3-quart saucepan. Add the mushrooms and cook for 5 minutes. Add the scallops. Cover and turn off the fire. Drain after 3 minutes, reserving the liquid.

Melt the butter in a double boiler. Add the shallots and cook over an open medium fire for 1 minute, then return to the double boiler. Add the flour and stir briefly. Add the scallop/mushroom liquid and cream.

While constantly whisking, add the egg yolks one at a time. Mix well, then add the sherry and salt and pepper to taste. Stir until the sauce is thick and creamy. Add the scallops and mushrooms and heat for 1 minute. Serve on buttered toast or rice. Sprinkle with chopped, crisp bacon and some chopped chives. Dust with paprika.

Curry of Seafood

8 servings

½ cup sweet butter
1 large onion, grated
1 large clove garlic, grated
3 ribs celery, grated
3 tablespoons all-purpose flour
2 cups Fish Stock (p. 25)
2 cups sour cream
1 cup banana, mashed
2 tablespoons curry powder
   (more or less, to taste)
½ teaspoon ground ginger

3 cups cooked lobster and/or
   shrimp, cut in bite-size pieces
cooked white rice,
   accompaniment
cayenne pepper, for garnish
parsley, chopped, for garnish
curry condiments (see Chicken
   Curry, p. 207), accompaniment
curry powder,
   accompaniment

Melt the butter in the top of a double boiler. Grate in the onion, garlic, and celery (or put in a blender with 2 tablespoons of Fish Stock, then put in the pot). Cook on an open medium fire for about 5 minutes, being careful not to burn. Return to the double boiler, then add the flour and mix well. Add the stock, sour cream, and banana. Stir briefly, then add the curry powder and ginger. Cook at least 20 minutes. Add the lobster and/or shrimp and heat through.

To serve, put a ring of rice on the plate, making a well in the center, then put some curry in the well. Garnish with sprinkles of cayenne pepper and chopped parsley. Pass bowls of the condiments and a shaker of curry powder.

Fettuccine with Crawfish

4 servings

8 quarts water	3 cloves garlic, minced
2 tablespoons salt	½ teaspoon cayenne pepper
¾ pound fresh fettuccine	1½ teaspoons salt
oil, to coat (optional)	1 chicken bouillon cube
3 tablespoons butter	3 tablespoons dry white wine
1 cup mushrooms, chopped	1 cup heavy cream
1 cup scallions, chopped	1 tablespoon (or more) Pesto
1 pound cleaned crawfish tails	Sauce (p. 184)
(or small, peeled shrimp)	dash Tabasco

In a large pot bring the water and salt to a boil. Add the fettuccine and boil for 2½ minutes. Drain and rinse the fettuccine briefly with cold water. Put into a large bowl so it can be tossed with the sauce later. This may be done several hours in advance, tossing with a little oil to prevent sticking.

Melt the butter in a deep skillet over medium-high heat. Add the mushrooms and scallions and sauté for 2 minutes. Throw in the crawfish tails. Sauté for 1 minute. Add the garlic, cayenne, salt, bouillon cube, and white wine and cook for 1 minute. Add the cream, Pesto Sauce, and Tabasco. Bring to a slow boil and reduce by cooking until the mixture is thick, about 3–5 minutes. Pour the sauce over the fettuccine and toss to coat. Divide among warm plates and serve immediately.

Flounder with Almonds or Lemon

There are many wonderful ways to prepare and serve flounder. Since it is so delicate, it is important never to overcook this fish. Here is a basic preparation, followed by a couple of ways to finish the dish.

4 servings

2 cups all-purpose flour

2 tablespoons salt

1 teaspoon white pepper

1 teaspoon mace

2 teaspoons dry mustard

3 tablespoons paprika

4 flounder fillets

butter, for sautéing

grated Parmesan cheese, on top

Combine the dry ingredients, then dust the flounder fillets. Sauté the rounded side first in butter for 3 minutes. Carefully turn the fish. Sprinkle with grated Parmesan cheese. Cook for 2 minutes, then remove to a warm plate or platter. (Do not clean the skillet just yet.)

Flounder Amandine

½ cup butter

¼ cup sliced toasted almonds

¼ cup dry white wine

3 tablespoons lemon juice

Heat the butter in the same skillet, then add the almonds. Sauté for 1 minute, then pour over the fish. Add the wine and lemon juice to the skillet over high heat. Cook for a minute or two, scraping the pan to loosen the scraps, then pour over the fish. Sprinkle with chopped parsley and garnish with wedges of lemon and sprigs of parsley.

Flounder with Lemon

2 tablespoons butter
3 tablespoons lemon juice
1 cup dry white wine
12 thin slices lemon
parsley sprigs, for garnish
lemons, for garnish

Add the butter, lemon juice, and wine to the skillet. Reduce by cooking to half, then add the lemon slices. Simmer for a couple of minutes. Arrange the lemon slices on top of the fish attractively. Pour the hot butter and wine mixture over the fish. Sprinkle with chopped parsley and garnish with wedges of lemon and sprigs of parsley.

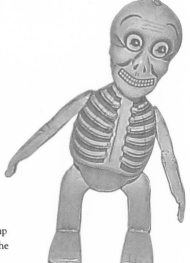

This was one of Tom's favorite wind-up toys. He thought it wobbled just like he did when his knees were hurting.

Flounder Mornay

Flounder Mornay

There are many combinations that work well with Flounder in Mornay Sauce. Below are 3 good variations. Experiment!

1 serving

1 cup Mornay Sauce (p. 183)
2 small flounder fillets
¼ cup grated Parmesan cheese
paprika, for color
chopped parsley, for garnish

Coat the bottom of a casserole or an individual baking dish with some Mornay Sauce. Roll up the flounder fillets and place in the dish. Spoon in more Mornay Sauce, covering the fish. Sprinkle with the cheese and dust with paprika. Bake at 450° until the sauce bubbles and is golden brown. Serve either in the hot casserole or remove to a warmed plate. Sprinkle with chopped parsley. Serve with rice and a green vegetable.

Variation 1

½ cup cooked lobster and/or crabmeat
12 (or more) white grapes

After putting the fillets in the baking dish add the above ingredients. Cover with more Mornay Sauce and finish off as above.

Variation 2

½ cup cooked shrimp, peeled and deveined
12 (or more) orange sections, membrane removed
¼ cup cooking brandy

Arrange cooked shrimp on top of the flounder. Cook the orange sections briefly in the brandy over medium heat, then add to the casserole. Cover with Mornay Sauce and finish as above.

Variation 3

½ cup cooked spinach, drained well
1–3 thin slices tomato

Put the spinach in the dish, then the fish. Cover with Mornay Sauce. Place the tomato slices on top, then finish as above. This dish could be called Flounder Florentine.

Flounder with Tomatoes and Olives

4 servings

4 flounder fillets
2 cups green and black olives, chopped
2 tablespoons butter
1 onion, grated
2 ribs celery, grated
½ clove garlic, grated
1 cup dry white wine
1 whole bay leaf
3 cups tomatoes, peeled (see Eggplant Provençal, p. 60), seeded, and chopped

1½ tablespoons fresh basil, chopped
1½ tablespoons parsley, chopped
1 teaspoon sugar
salt and pepper, to taste
mozzarella cheese, on top
Romano cheese, on top
olive halves, on top
chopped parsley, for garnish

Roll the fillets in the olives. Place in a casserole or individual baking dishes. Melt the butter in a 2-quart saucepan over medium heat, grate in the onion, celery, and garlic, then cook for 5 minutes. Add the wine and bay leaf and cook for 10 more minutes. Add the tomatoes, herbs, sugar, salt, and pepper. Cook for another 15 minutes or so, then pour over the fish. Finish off with dots of mozzarella cheese in the center and good sprinkles of Romano cheese and olive halves. Bake at 450° until the edges bubble and the top turns golden brown. Serve with sprinkles of chopped parsley.

Flounder with Anchovy Butter

1 serving

½ soft butter
6 anchovy fillets, finely minced
   or mashed
3 tablespoons lemon juice
pinch onion powder
small pinch cayenne pepper
1 flounder fillet

1 tablespoon bread crumbs
1 tablespoon grated Parmesan
   cheese
2 tablespoons Maître d'Hôtel
   Butter (p. 26)
lemon, for garnish
parsley sprigs, for garnish

Combine the butter, anchovies, lemon juice, onion powder, and cayenne pepper, then brush some on the flounder fillet. Place the fish in a casserole brushed with a little of the anchovy butter. Sprinkle with a mixture of the bread crumbs and grated cheese, then dot with bits of the anchovy butter. Bake at 425° for 15 minutes or until the fish flakes and loses its transparency.

Serve on a heated plate or, if the fish is large and is to be shared, on a hot platter. Top with a generous spoonful of Maître d'Hôtel Butter. Garnish with lemon wedges and parsley sprigs.

Lamb Curry

8 servings

1 seven- to eight-pound leg of lamb	1 tablespoon paprika
2 celery ribs, quartered	2 cups onions, finely minced
1 small onion, quartered	1 cup green peppers, finely minced
2 cloves garlic, whole	3 cloves garlic, finely minced
2 carrots, quartered	2 jalapeño peppers, finely minced
4 beef bouillon cubes	1 cup carrots, finely minced
2 tablespoons (more or less, to your taste) curry powder	1 cup celery, finely minced
2 cups all-purpose flour	3 apples, grated
1 teaspoon dry mustard	1 cup raisins
½ teaspoon thyme	1 cup pineapple juice
½ teaspoon white pepper	1 cup apple juice
½ teaspoon chili powder	melted butter, for thickening
1 tablespoon onion powder	chopped parsley, for garnish
1 tablespoon salt	

Have the leg of lamb boned, saving the fat and the bone. Put the bone in a 1-quart stock pot and cover with water. Add the celery, onion, garlic, carrots, and bouillon cubes. Cook over medium heat for 2 hours. Strain and reduce by cooking to 2 cups of liquid.

Combine the flour and spices (except the curry powder). Cut the lamb leg into 1-inch cubes and sprinkle with the curry powder, then sprinkle with the seasoned flour, saving a little for thickening later.

In a heavy pot with a lid or a Dutch oven melt the lamb fat and then brown the meat. Remove the meat and add the finely minced vegetables, apples, and raisins. Sauté everything for a few minutes, then stir in the juices.

Return the meat to the pot, cover, and put into a 350° oven for 45 minutes or until the lamb is tender (don't overcook!). The liquid should be thick enough to coat a spoon. If not, thicken it with butter and seasoned flour mixed in equal parts. Garnish with sprinkles of chopped parsley. Serve with saffron rice and green peas. Pass a tray of condiments (see Chicken Curry, p. 207).

Lobster Mornay

4 servings

2–3 cups lobster meat, boiled or steamed, in bite-size pieces
4 cups hot Mornay Sauce (p. 183)
½ cup bread crumbs
½ cup grated Parmesan cheese
paprika, for color
cooked rice or toast triangles, crust removed, accompaniment
parsley sprigs, for garnish

Put the lobster meat in individual baking dishes or one large casserole, then pour over the hot Mornay Sauce. Sprinkle with the bread crumbs and Parmesan cheese, and dust with paprika. Place under the broiler until the top turns golden brown. Serve over rice or toast triangles. Garnish with parsley sprigs.

Grilled Garlic Shrimp

Grilled Garlic Shrimp

4 servings

32 very large shrimp, with shells and tails on
6 tablespoons olive oil
8 tablespoons paprika
2 tablespoons salt
4 teaspoons cayenne pepper
½ cup butter
3 cloves garlic, chopped
2 tablespoons parsley, chopped
cooked rice, accompaniment
chopped parsley, for garnish

Remove the heads and legs from the shrimp. Slice lengthwise through the belly of each shrimp. Snap the backs so they lay flat, then arrange in rows on a baking sheet. Dribble the oil over them, then sprinkle on the paprika, salt, and cayenne pepper. Refrigerate for 1 hour.

Melt the butter in a small saucepan, then add the garlic. Sauté for 2 minutes and remove from the heat. Stir in the parsley and set aside.

Cook the shrimp in rows on a very hot grill (or in 1 or 2 large, heavy skillets), flesh side down, for 3 minutes. Turn onto their backs and cook another 2 minutes. Remove and arrange on beds of rice. Pour the garlic butter on top. Serve immediately with sprinkles of chopped parsley.

This can be messy, so have plenty of napkins handy.

Lobster Newburg

6 servings

½ cup sweet butter
3 tablespoons all-purpose flour
½ teaspoon dry mustard
1 tablespoon paprika
¼ teaspoon cayenne pepper
½ teaspoon salt
1 cup milk
1 cup heavy cream
1 cup cooking sherry
2 dashes Tabasco

6 egg yolks
1 "pony" (small cordial glass)
   good brandy
2 pounds lobster meat, boiled
   or steamed, in chunks
cooked rice or toast triangles,
   crust removed, accompaniment
parsley sprigs, for garnish

Melt the butter in the top of a double boiler. Stir in the dry ingredients, then add the milk, cream, ½ cup of the sherry, and Tabasco. Cook for 20 minutes, remove from the fire, and allow to cool.

In a large bowl beat the egg yolks until frothy. While still whisking, pour in the cooled cream sauce. Mix well, then return it to the double boiler. Add another ½ cup (or less, according to taste) of sherry and the brandy and cook for 5 minutes. Add the lobster meat. Cook for 3 minutes, stirring often, and taste for seasonings. Serve on beds of rice or over toast triangles and garnish with sprigs of parsley.

Louisiana Chicken with
Andouille and Artichoke Hearts

8 servings

1 pound andouille sausage,*
  cut into ½-inch cubes
3 pounds chicken breasts,
  cut into 1-inch cubes
1½ cups Seasoned Flour
  (p. 27)
bacon fat or butter, for frying
  (if necessary)
1 cup vegetable oil
1 cup celery, diced
2 cups onions, diced
2 cloves garlic, chopped
½ cup carrots, diced
1 cup green peppers, diced
1 cup red peppers, diced

1 jalapeño pepper, seeded and
  chopped (optional)
2 cups heavy cream
2 dashes Tabasco
2–3 cups rich Chicken Stock
  (p. 24)
cornstarch, for thickening
2 cans artichoke hearts,**
  drained and quartered
bread crumbs (optional)
paprika (optional)
cooked rice, accompaniment
chopped scallion tops, for garnish

Brown the andouille in a 1-gallon, heavy-bottomed pot. Remove to the side. Dust the chicken cubes with ½ cup of the Seasoned Flour. Brown the cubes lightly in the same pot, adding bacon fat or butter when necessary to keep it from sticking or burning. Remove to the side.

Heat the oil in the same pot over medium heat. Add the rest of the Seasoned Flour, stirring constantly until the mixture is light brown (called a roux). Add the celery, onions, garlic, and carrots. Cook for a few minutes, then add the peppers and, if you like, the jalapeño pepper. Cook for a few more minutes, stirring often.

Add the cream, Tabasco, and stock. Heat for a few minutes and, if necessary, thicken with cornstarch mixed with water. If it's too thick, add some more stock. Taste for seasonings. Add the chicken, andouille, and artichoke bottoms (also called hearts) and mix well.

Put into a 350° oven and bake for 45 minutes or until the chicken is done. (Or transfer the mixture to an ovenproof casserole, top with bread crumbs, and dust with paprika. Finish as above.) Serve with rice and sprinkles of chopped scallion tops.

*If andouille is unavailable, use a good quality smoked, spiced sausage.

**Use artichoke bottoms canned in water, not marinated in oil. Or, better yet, use freshly cooked artichoke bottoms (see Hot or Cold Artichokes, p. 68).

An early painting of Tom by Ben Morris

Panéed Garlic Fish

Panéed Garlic Fish

4 servings

8 heads Roasted Garlic (p. 88)
water or chicken broth
4 eight-ounce firm-textured fish
   fillets (drum, snapper, redfish,
   etc.)
1 cup bread crumbs
⅛ teaspoon paprika
⅛ teaspoon dry mustard
⅛ teaspoon ground thyme
⅛ teaspoon onion powder
⅛ teaspoon white pepper

⅛ teaspoon salt
pinch chili powder or ground
   cumin (optional)
1 beaten egg
½ cup milk
paprika, for color
¼ cup clarified butter (see
   Barbecued Shrimp, p. 39)
   or salad oil
lime wedges, for garnish

Prepare the Roasted Garlic. After it cools, squeeze the garlic out and puree it in a food processor or put through a sieve. It should be the consistency of heavy mayonnaise. If it is too thick to spread, add a little water or chicken broth. This should yield ½–¾ cup.

Smear the roasted garlic puree over both sides of the fish. Combine the bread crumbs with the herbs and spices. Dip each fillet into a mixture of the egg and milk. Coat with the seasoned bread crumbs. Dust the rounded side (the side that will be cooked first) with a little paprika for color.

Heat the clarified butter or oil in a skillet large enough to comfortably hold the fish (or use 2 pans). Sauté the fish over medium heat (carefully, so as to not burn the bread crumbs) for 2–5 minutes per side, depending on the thickness of the fish fillets. Total cooking time should be approximately 10 minutes per inch of thickness, measured at the thickest point. If a thick fish is used, sauté until the coating takes on color, then transfer to a 400° oven to finish cooking. Garnish with wedges of lime. Serve with one or more of the following salsas on the side: Carrot and Red Pepper with Pecans (p. 168); Garlic and Orange (p. 176); Mango, Peach, and Apple (p. 180); or Tomatillo (p. 191).

Poached Salmon with Hollandaise

4–6 servings

1 whole small salmon fillet or 4–6 five- to eight-ounce salmon steaks	1 whole bay leaf
	3 whole black peppercorns
	½ lemon, cut in rings
1–2 quarts Fish Stock (p. 25) or a combination of:	pinch salt
	softened butter
1–2 quarts water	watercress sprigs, for garnish
2–3 dashes (more or less, to taste) Tabasco	lemon wedges, for garnish
	2–3 cups hollandaise

Wrap the salmon in cheesecloth and put it into a large pan. Cover with Fish Stock, bring to a boil, then reduce to a simmer. Cook until the fish flakes easily, about 30 minutes (more or less, depending on the size of the fish).

When it is done, lift the fish from the liquid with great care, unwrap it, and transfer it to a hot platter. Brush with butter. Garnish with sprigs of watercress and wedges of lemon. Pass a gravy boat of hollandaise.

Boiled small new potatoes tossed in a little butter and chopped fresh dill go well with this.

Roast Long Island Duck

This recipe can be done in one day, but it is easier to do in two.

6 servings

---

3 four- to five-pound Long Island ducklings

3 tablespoons leaf thyme

1 tablespoon black pepper, crushed (not ground)

3 tablespoons garlic salt (kosher salt with fresh garlic crushed into it)

saffron rice, accompaniment

vegetable, accompaniment

Duck Sauce* (p. 172)

sautéed cherry tomatoes, for garnish

parsley, for garnish

watercress, for garnish

Day One

Thaw well, if frozen, and rinse the ducks thoroughly. Trim each duck by removing the wing tips, leg ends, neck skin, and tail point (known in Tom's kitchen as "the pope's nose"!). Also remove the neck, liver, and gizzard from the cavity.**

Rub the ducks inside and out with the thyme, crushed pepper, and garlic salt. Place them breast side up on racks in a roasting pan and roast at 400° for 20 minutes, basting once or twice to keep the meat from drying out and to crisp the skin. Prick all over with a fork and cook for 20 more minutes.

Turn the ducks breast side down, prick, and cook for another 20–25 minutes, basting once or twice, or until the skin under the wings is brown. Remove from the pan and allow to cool, then refrigerate. Save the pan drippings for making sauces.

Day Two

When cool, cut the ducks in half lengthwise (a pair of good scissors works well) through the breastbone and then along both sides of the backbone, removing it. Carefully remove the ribs and other bones, leaving only the leg, thigh, and wing bones. Place the split ducks cut side down on racks in a roasting pan and roast in a 425° oven for 20 minutes, or until the skin is brown and crisp. Serve on a bed of saffron rice with the vegetable of your choice (peas, carrots, or green beans work). Pour some sauce on the duck and serve a gravy boat of extra sauce. Garnish with sautéed cherry tomatoes, sprinkles of chopped parsley, and sprigs of watercress or parsley.

*Duck Sauces include Fig, Ginger Peach, Orange, Plum, and Port (p. 172)

**These parts can be put into the roasting pan with the ducks, cooked separately to make a base for sautéed vegetables or tiny potatoes, or used in making a stock for sauces.

Hot Tip: Boning ducks is easier to do the second day, when they've had some time to "set."

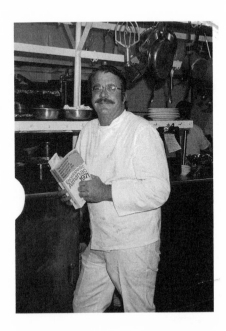

Rolatine of Chicken

Rolatine of Chicken

6 servings

3 half-pound boneless chicken breasts	⅛ teaspoon onion powder
12 slices cooked ham, thinly sliced	½ cup Romano cheese, grated
	1 cup milk
12 slices Swiss cheese (Provolone can be used)	2 eggs, beaten
	paprika, for color
1 pound fresh spinach, cleaned and steamed	butter
	½ cup cooking sherry
1 cup bread crumbs	2 cups Dijon Sauce (p. 170)
⅛ teaspoon salt	Rémoulade Sauce (optional)
⅛ teaspoon white pepper	(p. 187)
⅛ teaspoon powdered thyme	Dill Mayonnaise (optional) (p. 107)

Place the chicken breasts skin side up (but remove the skin) between 2 pieces of waxed paper and pound them to ¼-inch thickness. Remove the waxed paper and place them skin side down. On each one put a slice of ham, a slice of Swiss cheese, and finally some cooked spinach. Combine the bread crumbs, seasonings, and grated cheese. Roll up the chicken breasts, dip them in the milk mixed with the eggs, and roll them in the seasoned bread crumbs. Sprinkle with paprika to give color.

Butter a casserole or roasting pan large enough to hold the rolatines. Put in the rolatines and pour in the sherry. Bake in a 350° oven for 30 minutes, basting 2 or 3 times, adding more sherry or water, if necessary. When ready to serve, carefully slice the rolatines and arrange attractively on a plate. Pour hot Dijon sauce along one side (don't obscure the design). Serve with a small salad and extra Dijon sauce on the side.

This may be made a day ahead of time and reheated or served cold with mustard, Rémoulade Sauce, or Dill Mayonnaise.

Lobster Provençal

6 servings

2 or 3 one-and-one-half- or
   two-pound lobsters,* boiled
   or steamed
½ cup sweet butter
1–2 cloves garlic, crushed
¾ cup onions, finely chopped
¼ cup celery, finely chopped
½ cup fresh basil, finely chopped
3 cups tomatoes, peeled (see
   Eggplant Provençal, p. 60),
   seeded, and chopped

1 cup red wine
   (Burgundy, Chianti)
3 anchovy fillets, mashed
½ teaspoon sugar
salt and pepper, to taste
½ cup green and/or black
   olives, pitted
chopped parsley, for garnish

Remove the lobster meat from the shells, cut it into bite-size pieces, and set aside. Melt the butter in a 2-quart pot or deep skillet. Add everything except the olives and lobster meat. Cook over medium heat for 30 minutes or until it thickens. Now add the olives and cook 10 more minutes. Put the lobster meat on warm plates and pour over the very hot tomato sauce. Sprinkle with chopped parsley. Serve with saffron rice and peas.

*Number and size varies according to availability and how rich you are.

Roast Duck with Red Wine Garlic Sauce

6 servings

3 four- to five-pound ducks, trimmed

2 tablespoons garlic, chopped

½ cup kosher salt

6 tablespoons leaf thyme

2 tablespoons coarsely ground pepper

3 tablespoons Dijon mustard

½ cup soy sauce

4 heads garlic, split

6 carrots, cut in thirds

½ bunch celery, coarsely chopped

1 cup onions, chopped

3 whole bay leaves

8 cups water

1½–2 cups good red wine (Beaujolais, Burgundy)

½ cup cornstarch

salt and pepper, to taste

watercress sprigs, for garnish

chopped parsley, for garnish

Prepare the ducks (see Roast Long Island Duck, p. 236), saving the trimmings. Mix together the garlic, kosher salt, 3 tablespoons of thyme, and pepper. Rub the insides of the ducks with mustard. Rub the outsides with soy sauce. Sprinkle half of the salt mixture in the cavities. Stuff the ducks with 3 garlic heads, 3 tablespoons of thyme, 3 carrots cut in thirds, and half of the celery and place breast side up on racks in a roasting pan. Sprinkle the other half of the salt mixture on the outsides.

Roast at 425° for 45 minutes, basting occasionally. Turn the oven down to 350° and prick the breasts. Turn the ducks over and cook for another 45 minutes, basting again. Remove to cool.

While the ducks are cooking, make a stock (see Duck Stock, p. 172) by combining the trimmings, 1 head of garlic, 3 carrots cut in thirds, onions, the rest of the celery, bay leaves, and water in a 3-quart saucepan. Put on a low fire and simmer for about 1½ hours, or until it is reduced to 2 or 3 cups. Strain the stock and keep it warm.

When the ducks are done, remove them from the pan, pour off most of the fat, and place the pan over a medium fire. Add most of the wine and scrape the pan (deglaze). Mix the cornstarch with the rest of the wine to form a smooth paste, and pour some of it into the roasting pan. Add the strained Duck Stock, stir, and simmer for about 10 minutes. The sauce should be nicely thickened. If not, add a bit more cornstarch paste. Cook until the taste of cornstarch is gone. Taste for salt and pepper.

Split and bone the ducks (see Roast Long Island Duck, p. 236) or carve at the table. Pour on a little sauce and pass a gravy boat with more sauce. Garnish with watercress and sprinkles of chopped parsley. Serve with rice and your favorite vegetable.

Roast Goose with Apple and Prune Stuffing

8–12 servings

3 quarts water	2 cups dried prunes
1 large onion, cut up	8 cups dry bread, cubed
2 ribs celery, cut up	1 eight- to twelve-pound goose
2 whole bay leaves	leaf thyme
2 whole cloves garlic	black pepper
1 bunch (6–8 sprigs) parsley	garlic, crushed into kosher salt
3 chicken bouillon cubes	1 cup all-purpose flour
the goose neck and giblets	2 tablespoons red pepper or
(liver and gizzard)	currant jelly
¼ cup butter	1 cup good red wine
2 cups onions, chopped	(Beaujolais)
1 cup green peppers, chopped	cornstarch, for thickening
1 cup celery, chopped	(if necessary)
2 cups apples, diced	salt, to taste

Start the giblet gravy before preparing the goose. Combine the water, onion, cut-up celery, bay leaves, garlic, parsley, bouillon cubes, neck, liver, and gizzard in a 1-gallon pot and let simmer while the goose is cooking. About an hour before the goose is ready, strain the liquid into another pot and over a high flame reduce by half to make a rich stock. Save the giblets and chop them when cool.

Melt the butter in a 3-quart pot over medium heat. Add the chopped onions, peppers, chopped celery, apples, and prunes. Cook until the onions are transparent, then add the bread. The stuffing should be moist, not dry. Add some water or stock, if necessary.

Rub the goose with the thyme, pepper, and garlic salt. Prick the goose all over, then stuff the bird and place breast side down in a roasting pan with a rack. Roast at 325° for 3½ to 4½ hours, turning the bird breast side up halfway through. Prick from time to time and drain off the drippings, saving about ½ cup for the gravy. If crisp skin is desired, sprinkle the bird with cold water 10 minutes before it is to come out of the oven. Remove the goose to a warm platter and keep warm while the gravy is made.

After the goose is done and removed, put the roasting pan on the stove over medium heat. Add the flour and drippings and stir well, scraping the pan. Slowly add the rich stock, then the jelly and wine. Cook until the flour taste is gone. If necessary, thicken with corn-starch mixed with red wine. Add the giblets and taste for salt.

Here is a sample menu using Roast Goose:

Christmas Dinner—1983

Baked Oysters with Garlic
Roast Goose with Apple and Prune Dressing—Giblet Gravy
Mashed Potatoes and Rutabaga
Spicy Red Cabbage
Steamed Broccoli with Hollandaise
Homemade Yeast Rolls—Red Pepper Jelly
Boston Lettuce Hearts—Dijon Vinaigrette
Montrachet Cheese
Pumpkin and Rum Mousse
Coffee
Served with lightly chilled Beaujolais

Salmon Steaks with Hot Caper Sauce

2 servings

3 or 4 slices onion
2 whole bay leaves
1 cup butter, softened
2 salmon (or swordfish) steaks, cut 1 inch thick
paprika, for color
1 cup Hot Caper Sauce (p. 178)

Put the onions and bay leaves in the butter and let stand for a few minutes, then generously brush it on the steaks. Sprinkle with paprika and broil for 3 minutes on one side. Turn and brush with the butter and broil another 5 minutes. Remove to hot plates and cover with Hot Caper Sauce.

Sautéed Bay Scallops

Tom wrote, "I personally think this is the best way to serve the deliciously sweet bay scallop. Don't cook too many at a time in the skillet and, most important, don't overcook!"

1 serving

¼ cup Seasoned Flour (p. 27)

¼–⅓ pound bay scallops

2 tablespoons butter

paprika, for color

chopped parsley, for garnish

lemon wedges, for garnish

Put the Seasoned Flour in a paper bag. Add the scallops and shake the bag to evenly coat. Melt the butter in a large skillet over medium-high heat. Heat the butter until it just begins to turn brown. Add the scallops (a few at a time), then dust with paprika. Sauté, shaking the pan, until the scallops are golden brown, about 3 minutes. Remove to a hot plate, sprinkle with chopped parsley, and garnish with a wedge of lemon.

Sautéed Blowfish

Tom wrote, "The blowfish (or sea squab) is a delicious fish and easy to prepare. It only has a single backbone, so it is also easy to eat. The fish is small so plan on 3 or 4 per person."

4 servings

12–16 blowfish, cleaned*	1 teaspoon mace
1 cup cornmeal	milk
1 cup cracker crumbs	peanut oil, for frying
1 teaspoon salt	lemon wedges, for garnish
1 teaspoon pepper	parsley, for garnish
1 tablespoon paprika	broiled tomatoes, for garnish

Wipe the fish with a damp cloth. Combine the dry ingredients. Dip the fish in milk, then roll in the cornmeal mixture. Heat ½ inch peanut oil in a skillet (do not allow to smoke) and fry the fish gently for 3 minutes on one side. Turn carefully and cook another 2 minutes. Remove and drain on paper towels. Serve with wedges of lemon, bunches of parsley, and broiled tomatoes.

See Blowfish in White Wine Sauce (p. 199).

*Be sure the liver and ovaries are removed as they are poisonous!

Seafood Paella

6 servings

½ cup sweet butter	12–18 small shrimp, peeled and deveined
¾ cup onions, finely chopped	12–18 mussels, well scrubbed and debearded (see Mussels in Garlic Sauce, p. 76)
½ cup celery, finely chopped	
1 clove garlic, chopped	
2½ cups uncooked rice	1 cup pimiento, chopped
1 teaspoon saffron	½ cup green olives, pitted
1 whole bay leaf	1 cup warm cooked lobster meat, chunked
2 cups (or more) boiling Chicken Stock (p. 24)	
1 cup clam juice	2 cups cooked peas
18 small clams, well scrubbed	chopped parsley, for garnish
1 pint scallops	chopped pistachio nuts, for garnish

Melt the butter over medium heat in a 6-quart casserole or earthenware pot with a lid. Add the onions, celery, and garlic and, stirring often, cook until transparent, about 5 minutes. Add the rice and stir for 1 minute. Add the saffron, bay leaf, stock, clam juice, and clams. Cover with waxed paper, then put on the lid.

Bake at 350° for 25 minutes. Remove from the oven and quickly stir in the scallops, shrimp, mussels, pimientos, and olives. If the rice is getting too dry, add some more of the boiling Chicken Stock. Cover and return to the oven for 15 minutes. Remove from the oven again, add the lobster meat and peas, and mix well. Empty onto a heated platter or serve from the casserole. Garnish with chopped parsley and chopped pistachio nuts.

Shrimp Curry

6–8 servings

¼ cup vegetable oil
2 cups onions, chopped
1 cup carrots, chopped
1 cup red bell peppers, chopped
1 cup yellow bell peppers, chopped
½ cup celery, chopped
¼ cup garlic, minced
¼ cup curry powder (more or less, to taste)
1½ cups Granny Smith apples, grated
1½ tablespoons fresh ginger, grated
1 Jalapeño pepper, chopped
1 cup apple juice
1 cup pineapple juice

1 tablespoon orange juice concentrate
1 quart shrimp stock (see Fish Stock, p. 25)
½ cup yogurt
2–4 tablespoons cornstarch, for thickening
3–4 pounds raw shrimp, peeled and deveined
cooked rice, accompaniment
peas, accompaniment
chopped cilantro, for garnish
parsley sprigs, for garnish
curry condiments (see Chicken Curry, p. 207), accompaniment

Heat the oil in a heavy, 6-quart pot over medium heat. Add the vegetables and cook until tender, about 6-7 minutes. Add everything but the cornstarch and shrimp. Thicken the sauce with cornstarch mixed with some of the liquid from the pot. Cook 30 minutes, or until the cornstarch taste is gone. Add the shrimp and cook another 5 minutes. Serve immediately with rice, peas, sprinkles of chopped cilantro, parsley sprigs, and the curry condiments.

Sweetbreads and Mushrooms en Brochette

6 servings

2 pounds sweetbreads
3 tablespoons tarragon vinegar
1 teaspoon salt
24 mushroom caps
18 small white onions
1 egg, beaten
½ cup milk or Half & Half

½ cup Seasoned Flour (p. 27)
oil, for deep frying
6 garlic croutons* or
   cooked rice
Dijon mustard, to taste
2–3 cups hollandaise

Wash the sweetbreads in warm water. Remove any obvious veins. Put into a 2-quart pot with the vinegar, water to cover, and salt. Bring to a boil. Reduce to a simmer and cook for 4–5 minutes. Drain, then rinse with cold water. Put the sweetbreads between 2 cookie sheets and weigh down to make firm. When cool, cut into squares and remove any tough fibers. Thread onto skewers: 1 mushroom cap, 1 piece sweetbread, 1 onion. Repeat 3 times, ending with a mushroom cap. Dip each brochette into a mixture of the egg and milk. Dust with Seasoned Flour and deep fry until golden brown. Place (skewers removed) on the croutons or beds of rice and mask with Dijon hollandaise (Dijon mustard mixed with hollandaise). Put under the broiler until the hollandaise takes on slight color.

*Garlic croutons are slices of crustless bread fried to a golden brown in olive oil in which garlic has been cooked.

Swordfish with Mussels
and Mushrooms

Swordfish with Mussels and Mushrooms

4 servings

4 five- to eight-ounce swordfish steaks

3–4 cups Court Bouillon (p. 217) or 3–4 cups Fish Stock (p. 25)

20–24 mussels, steamed and shelled (see Mussels in Garlic Sauce, p. 76)

16–20 small mushrooms, sautéed

3–4 cups Mornay Sauce (p. 183)

1 cup grated Parmesan cheese

paprika, for color

cooked rice, accompaniment

parsley, for garnish

lemon wedges, for garnish

Poach the steaks (see Seafood Cakes, p. 92) in Court Bouillon or Fish Stock for 10 minutes, or until almost done (don't overcook). Remove to individual baking dishes or one large casserole. Place the mussels and mushrooms around the fish. Cover with hot Mornay Sauce. Sprinkle with Parmesan cheese and dust with paprika. Put under the broiler until the sauce bubbles and browns. Serve with rice, sprinkle with chopped parsley, and garnish with parsley sprigs and lemon wedges.

Swordfish on a Sword

Swordfish on a Sword

4 servings

1 cup olive oil	small whole onions (optional)
½ cup white wine	whole mushrooms (optional)
½ cup cooking sherry	cooked rice, accompaniment
1 clove garlic, crushed	broiled tomatoes, accom-
1 onion, sliced	paniment
2 tablespoons soy sauce	English mustard, on the side
3 whole bay leaves	mayonnaise, on the side
2 pounds swordfish, cut into	dill, to taste
2-inch squares	lemon juice, to taste
pieces of parboiled* green	
pepper (optional)	

Prepare a marinade by combining the oil, wine, sherry, garlic, onion, soy sauce, and bay leaves. Cover it and refrigerate for at least 2 hours, overnight if possible. Put the squares of swordfish in the marinade 15 minutes before cooking time, turning 2 or 3 times. Remove and put on broiling skewers, alternating, if you wish, with the peppers, onions, and mushrooms. Broil over charcoal for 10 minutes or until done, basting with the marinade and turning often. Serve with rice, broiled tomatoes, English mustard, and mayonnaise mixed with chopped fresh dill and lemon juice.

*To parboil the peppers (or other vegetables) plunge them into rapidly boiling water, boil for about 2 minutes, drain, then rinse or put down in cold water to stop the cooking. This will preserve the color and nutrients and allow the vegetable to be fully cooked on the grill.

Tenderloin of Pork Cordon Bleu

6 servings

2 one-pound pork tenderloins

Dijon mustard

½ pound prosciutto, sliced very
thin

I pound Swiss cheese, sliced
thin

Seasoned Flour (p. 27)

I egg, beaten

½ cup milk

I cup bread crumbs

½ cup Romano cheese, grated

I chicken bouillon cube

I tablespoon sherry

I tablespoon shallots, minced

3 cups heavy cream

I tablespoon Dijon mustard

I tablespoon green
peppercorns, crushed

salt, to taste

butter, for sautéing

watercress, for garnish

Slice the tenderloins at an angle into ½-inch pieces, allowing 4 per serving, then butterfly (split, but don't cut all the way through) and flatten with a mallet or the side of a heavy knife.

Lay the tenders out and brush one side with Dijon mustard, put prosciutto and Swiss cheese slices between the butterflied pork pieces, then fold together. Pat with Seasoned Flour, dip in the egg mixed with milk, then coat with the bread crumbs mixed with grated Romano cheese. Refrigerate until ready to cook.

To make the green peppercorn sauce, in a heavy 1-quart saucepan dissolve the bouillon cube in the sherry, add the shallots and cream, and cook over high heat until it's reduced to 1½ cups. Stir in the mustard and peppercorns and taste for salt. Sauce should be creamy, not too thin.

Sauté the pork tenders in butter until golden brown, being careful not to burn, then put in a 350° oven for 15–20 minutes. Put two slices of the pork on one side of the plate and a line of the green peppercorn sauce along one side of the meat. Garnish with sprigs of watercress.

Broccoli, grilled tomatoes, and tiny roasted potatoes are very good with this dish.

Suggested wine: Beaujolais Nouveau or other light red wine.

Tournedos Thomas

4 servings

24 baby carrots, sautéed
¼ pound fresh spinach, sautéed
  just until wilted
24 cherry tomatoes, sautéed
butter, for sautéing
4 garlic croutons*
4 artichoke bottoms, quartered
  (see Hot or Cold Artichokes,
  p. 68)

2 cups (or more) Marchand de
  Vin Sauce (p. 181)
4 six- to eight-ounce filet
  mignon steaks
2 cups (or more) Béarnaise
  Sauce (p. 166)

Sauté the carrots, spinach, and tomatoes separately in butter. Place the croutons on plates, radially arrange the carrots and tomatoes around them, and put the spinach in the centers. Put the artichoke bottoms on the spinach, ladle Marchand de Vin Sauce over them, then put the plates in a 200° oven to heat. Cook the steaks to order, then put on top of the other ingredients. Spoon Béarnaise Sauce over each and serve immediately. Pass gravy boats of both sauces.

*Garlic croutons are slices of crustless bread fried to a golden brown in olive oil in which garlic has been cooked. Make these 1½ inches in diameter.

Tandoori Turkey Breast

Tandoori Turkey Breast

6 servings

1 three-pound turkey breast (or chicken breast)	1 two-inch piece fresh ginger, peeled and chopped
¼ teaspoon cayenne pepper	1¼ teaspoons cumin seeds
½ teaspoon salt	1 tablespoon coriander seeds
3 tablespoons lime juice	½ teaspoon mustard seeds
freshly ground pepper, to taste	½ teaspoon hot pepper flakes
¾ cup low-fat yogurt	2 tablespoons peanut oil
4 cloves garlic, chopped	chopped cilantro, for garnish
2 scallion tops, chopped	

Cut gashes on both sides of the turkey breast. Combine the cayenne, salt, lime juice, and pepper and rub into the meat. Let stand for at least 20 minutes. Blend everything else but the peanut oil and cilantro. Rub this into the meat. Wrap in plastic and refrigerate for 12 hours. When ready to cook, put on a rack in a pan and scrape all the marinade onto the breast. Drizzle with the peanut oil. Bake at 350° for 45–55 minutes. Remove to a plate and scrape any drippings. Garnish with chopped fresh cilantro.

Veal Curry

8–10 servings

5 pounds veal stew meat, cubed
1 cup Seasoned Flour (p. 27)
3 tablespoons curry powder
(more or less, to taste)
½ cup clarified butter (see
Barbecued Shrimp, p. 39)
or cooking oil
3 cups celery, chopped
2 cups red bell peppers, chopped
2 cups yellow bell peppers,
chopped
3 cups onions, chopped
3 tablespoons garlic, chopped
4 jalapeño peppers, seeded and
chopped
2¼ cups (3 six-ounce cans)
apple juice
2¼ cups (3 six-ounce cans)
pineapple juice

3 apples (preferably Granny
Smith), peeled and grated
4 cups rich veal stock (see Beef
Stock, p. 22) or 1 beef and
2 chicken bouillon cubes in
4 cups water
2 tablespoons orange juice
concentrate
3 tablespoons fresh ginger,
grated
1 cup sour cream or
plain yogurt
cornstarch (mixed with apple
juice), for thickening
cooked rice, accompaniment
chopped cilantro, for garnish
curry condiments (see Chicken
Curry, p. 207),
accompaniment

Cut the stew meat into 1½-inch cubes. Combine the Seasoned Flour
with the curry powder. Coat the cubes with the mixture, then brown
the meat in a 6-quart pot in butter or oil. Remove and set aside. Add
the celery, peppers, onions, and garlic to the pot. Sauté for 3 or 4 minutes. Add the jalapeños, juices, apples, stock, concentrate, ginger, and,
finally, the meat. Cook until the meat is tender, 45 minutes or more,
then remove from the stove. Stir in the sour cream or yogurt. If the
sauce is too thin, add some cornstarch mixed with apple juice. Serve
with rice and garnish with chopped fresh cilantro. Pass a tray of curry
condiments.

Desserts

Desserts

Almond Amaretto Cake

16–20 servings

Cake

1 cup butter
2 cups sifted sugar
½ teaspoon vanilla extract
2 teaspoons almond extract
3 cups cake flour
½ teaspoon salt
2 teaspoons baking powder
1 cup milk
6 egg whites

Icing

2 cups butter
1½ pounds (about 5½ cups) confectioners' sugar, sifted
2 teaspoons almond extract
1 teaspoon vanilla extract
2 teaspoons orange juice concentrate
2 teaspoons lemon juice
1 cup Amaretto
½ cup slivered almonds, toasted

In an electric mixer whip the butter until light and fluffy. Add the sugar and blend well. Stir in the vanilla and almond extracts. In another bowl sift together the cake flour, salt, and baking powder. Stir ⅓ of this into the butter and sugar mixture. While stirring, add half of the milk. Add another ⅓ of the flour mixture, then the rest of the milk, then the rest of the flour mixture. Mix well. Whip the egg whites until stiff but not dry. Gently fold them into the cake mixture. Divide the mixture equally into three 9-inch cake pans that have been buttered and lightly floured.

Bake at 350° until the cakes are firm, about 25–30 minutes. The cakes are done when a toothpick stuck in the middle comes out clean. Place the pans on cake racks and let stand for 10 minutes. Invert the pans onto the racks and tap the pan bottoms to loosen the cakes. You may have to run a knife around the edges. Cool the layers completely (but don't let them dry out).

To make the icing, whip the butter in the electric mixer until it is light and fluffy. Slowly add the confectioners' sugar, extracts, orange juice concentrate, and lemon juice and blend until smooth.

When the cake is cool, place 1 layer on a cake plate. Prick the layer all over with a fork, sprinkle with ⅓ of the Amaretto, then ice the layer. Repeat the operation for the next 2 layers. Finish icing the cake and decorate, if desired, with toasted slivered almonds.

This is a very rich cake that will serve up to 20 people.

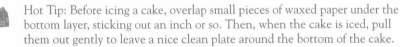

Hot Tip: Before icing a cake, overlap small pieces of waxed paper under the bottom layer, sticking out an inch or so. Then, when the cake is iced, pull them out gently to leave a nice clean plate around the bottom of the cake.

Almond Amaretto Mousse

8–10 servings

1 cup sugar
½ cup butter
4 eggs, separated
½ cup Half & Half
½ teaspoon vanilla extract
1 teaspoon almond extract
2 tablespoons Amaretto
1 tablespoon lemon juice
1 pint heavy cream
whipped cream, for garnish
slivered almonds, for garnish

Put the sugar, butter, egg yolks, and Half & Half in a heavy, 2-quart saucepan over medium heat. Stir constantly until it comes to a slow rolling boil. Let boil for 2 minutes, still stirring constantly. Remove from the heat. Strain into a bowl and put down into a larger bowl of ice. Continue stirring until the mixture is cool. Add the extracts, Amaretto, and lemon juice and mix well. Whip the heavy cream, then fold it into the mixture. Whip the egg whites until stiff (not dry), then fold them in. Fill wine or champagne glasses with the mixture. Cover with plastic wrap and chill until ready to serve. When serving, put dabs of whipped cream on top and sprinkle with slivered almonds.

English Custard

English Custard

Serve this with the famous Chocolate Cake (p. 270).
About 2½ cups

½ cup sugar
1 cup Half & Half
⅔ cup heavy cream
3 egg yolks
2 teaspoons cornstarch
1 teaspoon vanilla extract

Heat the sugar, Half & Half, and cream in a double boiler until the sugar melts, then, whisking constantly, add the egg yolks one at a time. Cook for 10 minutes, still whisking. Dissolve the cornstarch in a little of the mixture, then whisk into the mixture. Cook until the cornstarch taste is gone, about 15 minutes. Remove from the heat and add the vanilla extract. Serve warm or chilled.

Tom with dear friend, actor Louis Edmonds

Apple and Cherry
Bread Pudding

8–10 servings

Bread Pudding

1½ cups dried cherries

6 tablespoons Jack Daniel's whiskey

3 tablespoons Myers's rum

4 Granny Smith apples, peeled and cubed

1 loaf stale French bread, crust removed

Custard Sauce

4 eggs	butter, for sautéing
1½ cups sugar	3 tablespoons brown sugar
1 quart Half & Half	1 cup heavy cream, whipped
1 teaspoon vanilla extract	1 tablespoon brown sugar
1 teaspoon cinnamon	1 teaspoon vanilla extract
6 Granny Smith apples, peeled and cubed	2 Granny Smith Apples, grated

Soak the cherries in the bourbon and rum for 2 hours. Peel and cube 4 apples and mix with the soaking cherries. Cut the bread into 1½ to 2-inch squares. (If stale bread isn't readily available, put fresh bread in the oven to dry out.)

To make the custard sauce, in an electric mixer whip the eggs until light and fluffy. Add the sugar and beat for 3 minutes. Add the Half & Half, vanilla, and cinnamon.

Put the bread in a lightly buttered 9x13-inch glass baking dish. Add the cherries, apples, and liquor. Pour in the custard and bake at 350° for 30 minutes or until the custard is firm.

While the custard is baking, peel and cube 6 more apples into large chunks. Sauté the apples in a little butter in a large skillet until they begin to caramelize. Sprinkle with some brown sugar and cook for a few more minutes. Don't overcook!

Remove the pudding from the oven and spread the sautéed apples on top. Serve warm with cream that has been whipped with the brown sugar, vanilla extract, and 2 grated apples.

Hot Tip: Always whip cream in a well chilled bowl and add the sugar, vanilla extract, and other flavorings after whipping the cream until it's *almost* to the desired stiffness. This cuts down on total whipping time considerably.

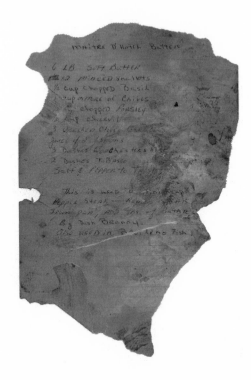

Banana Coconut Rum Cake

Banana Coconut Rum Cake

16–20 servings

Cake

1 cup butter

2 cups sifted sugar

½ teaspoon vanilla extract

2 teaspoons banana extract

3 cups cake flour

½ teaspoon salt

2 teaspoons baking powder

1 cup milk

6 egg whites

Icing

2 cups butter

1½ pounds (about 5½ cups) confectioners' sugar, sifted

2 teaspoons banana extract

1 teaspoon vanilla extract

2 teaspoons orange juice concentrate

2 teaspoons lemon juice

1 cup Myers's rum

1 banana, very thinly sliced

½ cup shredded coconut, toasted

To make the cake, in an electric mixer whip the butter until light and fluffy. Add the sugar and extracts and blend well. In another bowl sift together the cake flour, salt, and baking powder. Stir ⅓ of this into the butter and sugar mixture. While stirring, add half of the milk. Continue stirring and add another ⅓ of the flour mixture, then the rest of the milk, then the last of the flour mixture. Mix well.

Whip the egg whites until stiff but not dry. Gently fold them into the cake mixture. Divide the mixture equally into three 9-inch cake pans that have been buttered and lightly floured. Bake at 350° until the cakes are firm, about 25–30 minutes. The cakes are done when a toothpick stuck in the middle comes out clean.

Place the pans on cake racks and let stand for 10 minutes. Invert the pans onto the racks and tap the pan bottoms to loosen the cakes. You may have to run a knife around the edges. Cool the layers completely, but don't let them dry out.

To make the banana cream icing, whip the butter in an electric mixer until light and fluffy. Slowly add the confectioners' sugar, extracts, orange juice concentrate, and lemon juice and blend until smooth. Keep in a cool place but don't refrigerate.

When the cake is cool, place 1 layer on a cake plate (be sure to see the Hot Tip for Almond Amaretto Cake, p. 258, about icing cakes). Prick the layer all over with a fork, sprinkle with ⅓ of the rum, then ice the layer. Cover the icing with thinly sliced bananas and sprinkle with shredded coconut that has been toasted to a nice golden brown. Repeat the operation for the second layer, and then the third, leaving the bananas off the top of the cake. Cover the entire cake with more toasted coconut.

Barbados Rum Trifle

16–20 servings

Custard

2 cups Half & Half	1 tablespoon vanilla extract
2 cups heavy cream	2 tablespoons Barbados rum
1 cup sugar	6 egg yolks (set whites aside)
6 tablespoons cornstarch, dissolved in	1 tablespoon butter, melted

Cake*

1 cup soft butter	3 cups cake flour
1 cup sugar	1 tablespoon baking powder
1 teaspoon almond extract	pinch of salt
½ teaspoon vanilla extract	1 cup milk
3 egg yolks	6 egg whites

Fruit

1 small pineapple, cubed	2 tablespoons lime juice
2 oranges, sliced	1 cup Barbados rum
2 bananas, sliced	shredded coconut
2 cups seeded grapes	raspberry jam or currant jelly
2 cups strawberries (save one perfect one for the top)	whipped cream, for garnish
any other fruit you like	slivered almonds, for garnish

To make the custard, heat the Half & Half, cream, and sugar in a double boiler. Combine the cornstarch, vanilla, and rum. When the cream/sugar mixture is hot, whisk in the cornstarch mixture and cook, stirring often, for 10–15 minutes or until the cornstarch taste is gone. Whisk in the egg yolks one at a time. Continue whisking and cook for 5 more minutes. Remove from the heat and stir in the melted butter.

To make the almond cake, in an electric mixer combine the butter, sugar, almond and vanilla extracts, and egg yolks and beat on high until creamy. Sift together separately the flour, baking powder, and salt. Add ⅓ of the flour mixture, then ⅓ of the milk, and so forth, to the creamed butter, mixing until all is incorporated and smooth. Whip the egg whites until stiff but not dry and gently fold into the mixture.

Divide into three 9-inch cake pans (the ones with removable bottoms are best) that have been buttered and lightly floured. Bake at 350° until done, about 25–30 minutes. The cake is done when a toothpick stuck in the middle comes out clean. Place the layers on wire racks to cool.

Mix the fruit in a large bowl and sprinkle with the lime juice and rum.

To assemble, use a clear, straight-sided, glass bowl, especially if the trifle is going to be presented. Put a layer of cake in the bottom of the bowl. Sprinkle with some of the rum from the soaking fruit. Put a layer of custard, then a layer of the mixed fruit. At this point, line the sides of the bowl with thin slices of orange (peel on) alternating with strawberries that have been cut in half (cut sides in). Continue to fill the bowl with alternating layers of cake, rum, custard, and fruit, with custard for the last layer. Sprinkle the top with shredded coconut, dot with some jam or jelly, then put a perfect strawberry in the middle. Refrigerate overnight, if possible.

When serving, dig down through the layers. Top off with dollops of whipped cream and sprinkles of slivered almonds.

*You may substitute stale white or gold cake or packaged pound cake.

Chocolate Mousse

10–12 servings

1 batch chocolate icing (see Chocolate Cake, p. 270)
¾ cup Myers's rum
1 quart heavy cream, whipped
12 egg whites, whipped until stiff, not dry
whipped cream, for decoration

Mix the icing and rum. Gently fold in the whipped cream and whipped egg whites. Put into champagne glasses, refrigerate for an hour or so, then serve with dabs of sweetened, whipped cream.

Tom and some staff members of the Colony Hotel in Palm Beach, Florida
(Not *all* protrusions are caused by the Chocolate Mousse!)

Cappuccino dell' Amore

Make the base for this after-dinner drink at least one day ahead.

About 16 servings

1 empty liquor bottle or other
   quart-size bottle
brandy
gin
rum
licorice liqueur
white crème de cacao
dark crème de cacao
2 or 3 cinnamon sticks
4 or 5 whole cloves

espresso coffee
grated, unsweetened chocolate,
   to taste
sugar, to taste
hot Half & Half, to taste
whipped cream
finely chopped almonds
shaved unsweetened or
   semi-sweet chocolate

Mix the liquors and liqueurs in equal parts in the bottle. Add the cinnamon sticks and cloves and let stand at least a few hours or overnight, if possible. When ready to serve put ¼ cup of the mix into each cappuccino cup or coffee mug and fill with espresso. Add grated chocolate, sugar, and Half & Half to your taste. Top with whipped cream, sprinkles of chopped almonds, and shaved unsweetened or semi-sweet chocolate.

Chocolate Cake

This recipe for Tom's famous Chocolate Cake was one of the few secrets that Tom kept. I don't think he ever knowingly gave the recipe to anyone. In fact, even I, his nephew, the "blood of his blood," had to get it indirectly from someone who surreptitiously wrote down the ingredients as he watched Tom making the cakes one day.

Only recently, however, I found out the ironic truth of the matter. The recipe was originally his mother's, and he stole it from her!

12–16 servings

Cake

1 cup water	1 cup buttermilk or sour cream
1 cup butter	1 tablespoon vanilla extract
4 one-ounce squares Baker's Unsweetened Chocolate	3 cups cake flour
	1 tablespoon baking powder
2 cups sugar	1 teaspoon baking soda
4 eggs	½ teaspoon salt

Icing*

6 one-ounce squares Baker's Unsweetened Chocolate	1 tablespoon orange juice concentrate
	instant coffee (optional mocha-flavored variation)
2 cups sugar	candied violets, for decoration (optional)
1 cup Half & Half	
1 cup butter	
4 egg yolks	English Custard (p. 261)
pinch of salt	bittersweet chocolate, for garnish
2 tablespoons vanilla extract	

To make the cake, put the water, butter, chocolate, and sugar in a double boiler and cook until the sugar is melted. Cool completely.

While this cools, start making the icing. Melt the chocolate in a double boiler or on a plate over a pan of boiling water. Combine the sugar, Half & Half, butter, egg yolks, and salt in a heavy, 2-quart saucepan. Stirring constantly, bring to a slow rolling boil. Stop stirring, reduce the heat, let it boil for exactly 2 minutes, then remove from the heat and strain into a large bowl. (At this point, this is a good base for other icings or for mousse.)

Add the melted chocolate, vanilla extract, orange juice concentrate, and the optional instant coffee, mixing well. Put the bowl into a larger bowl containing a layer of ice or refrigerate, stirring occasionally, until thick enough to spread.

When the cake mixture is cool, add the eggs, buttermilk or sour cream, and vanilla. Mix well. Sift together separately the flour, baking powder, baking soda, and salt. Gently fold this into the chocolate mixture until the flour is barely mixed in (don't beat). Divide the mixture into 3 buttered and floured 9-inch round cake pans.

Bake at 350° for 20–25 minutes, or until a toothpick comes out clean, then remove to racks to cool, being careful to assemble the cake before the layers dry out.

Ice the cake (see Hot Tip for Almond Amaretto Cake, p. 258) and decorate the top with candied violets. (Okay, this is optional!) Serve fairly thin slices (1–2 inches), pour a little English Custard around them, and shave some bittersweet chocolate over the custard.

*The icing makes a wonderful hot chocolate sauce for ice cream too.

Lastly, as my father had penciled in at the bottom of his copy of the recipe: "Make a dental appointment before eating!"

Orange Grand Marnier Mousse

12 servings

Mousse Base

1 cup sugar
½ cup heavy cream
½ cup butter
4 egg yolks (set aside the whites)

Mousse

1 teaspoon vanilla extract
2 tablespoons orange juice
   concentrate
½ cup orange marmalade
1 teaspoon lemon juice
½ cup Grand Marnier

grated rind of 2 oranges
½ cup heavy cream, whipped
4 egg whites, whipped
whipped cream, for garnish
grated orange peel, for garnish
Grand Marnier, for garnish

Combine the sugar, cream, butter, and egg yolks over medium heat in a heavy, 2-quart saucepan. Bring to a rolling boil, stirring constantly (don't let it burn or scorch). Let boil for 2 minutes, then strain into a bowl over ice.

When cool, whisk in the rest of the ingredients except the cream and egg whites. In 2 separate bowls whip the cream and whites until stiff. Gently fold the cream, then the egg whites, into the mixture. Fill champagne or wine glasses with the mousse, cover with plastic film, and let chill for 6 hours or more. When ready to serve, top with dabs of sweetened, whipped cream to which a little grated orange peel and a good dash of Grand Marnier has been added.

Peach Melba

6 servings

½ cup currant jelly
1 cup raspberries, sieved, or ½ cup red raspberry jelly
1 teaspoon cornstarch
⅛ teaspoon salt
½ cup sugar
1 tablespoon brandy

Bring the currant jelly and raspberry juice (or jelly) to a boil in a 3-cup saucepan. Separately mix the cornstarch, salt, sugar, and brandy. Add to the jelly mixture. Cook until the mixture is clear and thick. Remove from the heat, then chill well.

Put in order into each stemmed goblet with a large bowl:

2 scoops vanilla ice cream
1 scoop raspberry sherbet (centered on the vanilla)
4 fresh peach slices (around the sherbet)
¼ cup melba sauce (around the peaches)
generous dab sweetened, whipped cream
almond slivers
cherry on top

Yummy!

Pecan Pie

1 nine-inch pie

1 tablespoon flour
½ cup sugar
pinch salt
2 eggs
½ tablespoon vanilla extract
½ tablespoon butter, melted
1 cup dark Karo syrup
¾ cup pecans
1 nine-inch pie pastry (see Quiche [Basic], p. 84) or frozen pie shell
sweetened whipped cream or vanilla ice cream

Mix everything but the pecans in a bowl and beat well. Put the pecans into the pie shell and pour in the mixture. Bake in a preheated 450° oven for 15 minutes. Reduce heat to 350° and cook until puffed up and firm, about 30 minutes. Serve warm with dollops of whipped cream or ice cream.

 Hot Tip: Store-bought pie tins are okay in the microwave, for some reason. So, if the top of the pie begins to burn and the pie isn't done, put it in a microwave oven for 2–5 minutes on high to finish it off. Try it!

Pumpkin Mousse
with Rum

12 servings

1 cup sugar
½ cup heavy cream
½ cup butter
4 egg yolks (set aside the whites)
1½ cups pumpkin pie mix
1 teaspoon vanilla extract
1 teaspoon lemon juice

½ cup Myers's rum
½ cup heavy cream, whipped
4 egg whites, whipped
sweetened whipped cream,
    for garnish
grated orange peel, for garnish
rum, for garnish

Combine the sugar, cream, butter, and egg yolks in a heavy, 2-quart saucepan over medium heat. Bring to a slow rolling boil, stirring constantly (don't burn or scorch). Let boil for 2 minutes, then strain into a bowl over ice.

When cool, whisk in all but the cream and egg whites. In 2 separate bowls whip the cream and whites until stiff. Gently fold these into the mixture. Fill champagne or wine glasses with the mousse, cover with plastic film, and let chill for 6 hours or more. When ready to serve, top with dabs of sweetened whipped cream to which a little grated orange peel and a good dash of rum has been added.

Index

Chef Tom wearing one of his trademark bandanas

"I used to run into Chef Tom with some frequency in restaurants around town. I don't think there was another restaurateur I saw dining out as much. The odd and memorable thing about these encounters is that it always took me a few seconds to figure out who this friendly person greeting me was. Because when he went out, there was no better-dressed man than Tom Cowman."

-Thomas G. Fitzmorris, *The New Orleans Menu*, October 1994, p. 6.